KID PIX™ Around the World

A Multicultural Computer Activity Book

Written and illustrated by Barbara J. Chan

Addison-Wesley Publishing Company
Reading, Massachusetts Menlo Park, California New York
Don Mills, Ontario Wokingham, England Amsterdam Bonn
Sydney Singapore Tokyo Madrid San Juan
Paris Seoul Milan Mexico City Taipei

For Tobie Clare and children everywhere

Special thanks to:

Sue Gartley and Folk Art International in San Francisco, California, for great research support;

Steve Nelson, Janet Kalin, and the students at Valle Verde School in Walnut Creek, California: Mary, Carli, Joanna, Jessica, Elizabeth, Andrew, Sherri, Geoff, Lisa, Alex, Ashley, Bobby, Hubbell, Lauren, Trisha, Thomas, Drew, Chris, Christina, Tyler, Mike, Daniel, Jeff, Sheree, Kelli, Krystal, Steve, and Michelle; Christopher, Kevin, and Elaine Lowe of Healdsburg, California; and the folks at Brøderbund Software for enthusiastically testing the activities;

Kin Lam at Time Inc. for color prepress assistance, Ramona Mann for pronunciation research, Lisa Osta for color help, Melissa Padgett for design input, April Kerr and fellow children's book writers and illustrators for feedback and encouragement, the public and university libraries and librarians;

The people at Addison-Wesley: Sponsoring Editor Dave Rogelberg for a great idea and for appreciating my views on using computer technology to bridge the gaps between cultures; Project Editor Joanne Clapp Fullagar for guiding me through the labyrinth of creating this book; Kathy Traynor and Vicki Hochstedler for production support and guidance;

Kirin, Sonal, Kiki, Al, Joan, and Robert for Tobie care, and the many wonderful people from diverse cultures whom I met during my years at U.C. Berkeley's International House and during my travels to interesting places;

Phil Manfield for helping me uncover my dreams; James Kalin for technical and moral support, activity testing, and Tobie care; and my parents Ida and Ray Chan for instilling in me the love of books.

Library of Congress Cataloging-in-Publication Data

Chan, Barbara J.
Kid Pix around the world, a multicultural computer activity book
written and illustrated by Barbara J. Chan.
p. cm.
ISBN 0-201-62226-2
1. Intercultural education—United States—Computer-assisted instruction—Juvenile literature. 2. Education. Elementary—United States—Activity programs—Juvenile literature. 3. Social sciences—Study and teaching (Elementary)—United States—Juvenile literature. I. Title.
LC1099.3.C47 1993
370.19'6'0285--dc20

92-46141
CIP
AC

Sponsoring Editor David Rogelberg
Project Editor Joanne Clapp Fullagar
Production Editors Kathy Traynor, Vicki Hochstedler
Educational Reviewers Marsha Lifter, Rennie Mau, Merle L. Silverman, Cynthia R. Conway Waring, Rachel Wright
Cover Design Jean Seal
Book Design Barbara J. Chan
Set in 12–point Stone

1 2 3 4 5 6 7 8 9 10—BA—9796959493
First Printing, March 1993

CONTENTS

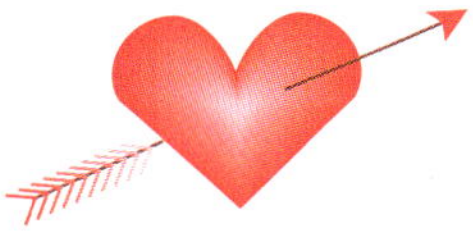

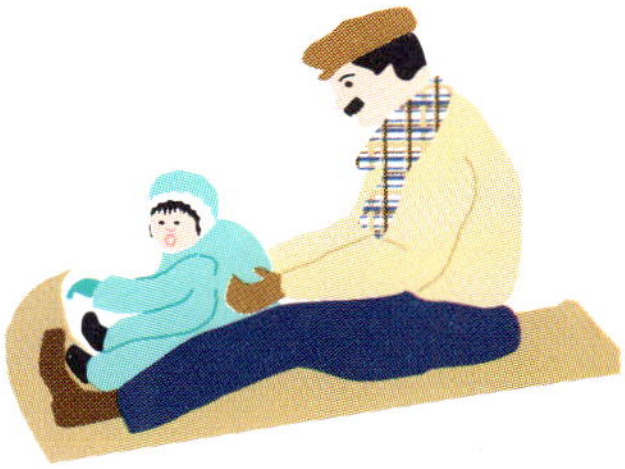

To Parents, Teachers, and Elders

K*id Pix Around the World* introduces twenty cultures through the joys of painting and drawing activities using Kid Pix. Readers are invited to travel to places around the world to learn about daily life, customs, and special traditions of different peoples and to explore and respond through related activities.

Each section focuses on a different culture and consists of two parts. The first part uses text and illustrations created with professional graphics programs to introduce some history. These passages focus on one custom or tradition and describe how customs may have originated, how they evolved, and how they are practiced today. In the second part, step-by-step text and Kid Pix pictures lead readers in using Kid Pix to explore and respond—first to draw or paint items similar to what they read about in the presented culture, and second, to create unique designs of their own.

The activities are designed to be guidelines rather than rigid prescriptions to be followed. Learning occurs through both spontaneous and guided exploration of Kid Pix features. Encourage readers to try each activity and celebrate serendipitous discoveries. While doing an activity, children may uncover other Kid Pix features and incorporate them into the activity. Congratulate them for being creative.

Here are a few suggestions for ways you can support a child's learning from ***Kid Pix Around the World.***

First, turn on Kid Pix and try painting your own picture. Read the Kid Pix manual so you can answer questions that the kids may ask. Then read "Around the World Toolkit" on page 6. Review new words in the Glossary and get ideas for supplementary reading materials from the Further Readings section at the end of this book.

You may want to read the cultural sketches aloud to preschoolers and beginning readers and discuss the passages and illustrations. Then describe the Kid Pix activity and show them the Kid Pix art examples in the step-by-step exercises. Turn on the computer and start Kid Pix. Point out the tool palette, show how to select different tools, and demonstrate how to navigate through the various options at the bottom of the screen. When needed, help children find the tools and guide little hands in holding down the Shift key as they draw circles.

Demonstrate how to make Rubber Stamps bigger by holding down appropriate keys as they stamp and how to use the Moving Van.

Younger readers may enjoy doing activities in pairs or small teams, taking turns reading the passages aloud and doing the steps in the activities. Teamwork encourages children to develop and use communication and cooperative learning skills. Older and younger children benefit from working together too. An older child may help a younger child with the writing activity in "Canciones" or "Pen Pals." While the younger child dictates the song or letter, the older child can type it on the computer. When it's time to illustrate the projects, they might take turns or each create an original drawing or painting—for example, his or her own family crest after reading about the Japanese kamon.

If you have a printer, you may help kids print and save their drawings and paintings. They might be used for the collage activity described near the end of the book.

You and your children may also enjoy learning more about different cultures. Together you might:

- Check out books from your local library to find out more about architecture, picture recordings, music, art, language, or customs in different cultures;
- Relate ***Kid Pix Around the World*** to school curricula. Kid Pix activities can be connected with literature, social studies and science, art, language, and cooking study units;
- Construct some of the objects described in the activities using available materials;
- Play music from different cultures to develop a feeling for a variety of sounds and rhythms;
- Learn about, make, and eat foods from different cultures. For example, make Chinese spring rolls on the day kids do the Tiger Slipper activity;
- Create costumes and write and perform a play. Make totem masks for a play about Pacific Northwest Indians.

The possibilities are unlimited when you and the kids let your imaginations range far and wide around the world.

Barbara J. Chan

Around the World Toolkit

You will need Kid Pix and a Macintosh, DOS, or Windows computer to do the activities in ***Kid Pix Around the World***. These items will be also useful:

printer and printer paper	tape
construction paper	scissors
cardboard	glue
safety pins	crayons
	string or ribbon

Please read the Kid Pix manual. Here are a few hints to help you use your version of Kid Pix while doing the activities.

In this book, Macintosh instructions are colored like this.

PC instructions are colored like this.

If a PC Windows instruction is different from PC DOS, it is colored like this.

Saving Your Drawings

To save your Kid Pix drawings, follow these steps. If you are using the Macintosh version,

1. Select Save from the File menu. A dialog box will appear.
2. Type the name of your drawing.
3. Click your mouse on the Save button. Kid Pix will save your drawing.

If you are using a DOS version,

1. Select Save from the File menu.
2. Choose the correct disk drive (a, b, c, or d).
3. Type the name of your drawing using 1-8 letters.
4. Click your mouse on the OK button.

If you are using the Windows version,

1. Select Save from the File menu.
2. Choose the correct disk drive (a, b, c, or d).
3. Click your mouse in the Save Changes To box.
4. Type the name of your drawing using 1-8 letters.
5. Click your mouse on the OK button.

Printing Your Drawing

Check to see if there is paper in the printer. If not, ask an adult to put in some paper. Turn the printer on or ask an adult to help you.

If you are using a Macintosh,

1. Select Print from the File menu or press Command-P. The Command key is the one with the curlicue symbol on it, next to the Spacebar.
2. When you see the Print dialog box, type the number of copies you want in the Copies box. Kid Pix will print that many copies of your drawing.
3. Click your mouse on the Print button. The printer will print your drawings.

If you are using a PC,

1. Select Print from the File menu. Kid Pix will automatically print one copy of your drawing.

Recording and Playing Sounds

You can record sounds if your Macintosh computer has a microphone. Follow the directions in the Kid Pix manual for recording sounds. You can save sounds with your drawings. Try the Canciones activity.

The DOS version of Kid Pix does not allow you to record sounds; however, the tools will make fun sounds with your PC speaker. If you have a sound card (Sound Blaster, Disney Sound Source, Tandy digital sound, or PS/1 Sound Option), you can hear the sounds that Kid Pix tools make or play the songs that are built into Kid Pix or hear the letters speak their names. Select Pick a Song from the Goodies menu to hear a song.

The Windows version requires Sound Blaster or an MPC-compatible Sound Card and a microphone in order for you to record and save sounds. You can Pick a Song from the Goodies menu to accompany one of your drawings.

Welcome to Kid Pix Around the World!

Have you ever wondered how people in different cultures live, what they eat, what they do, what they celebrate, and what they play? Come along with me as we travel around the world visiting people in such places as the Arctic, China, Japan, Switzerland, and Ghana.

Each chapter of this book tells you a little bit about a culture and suggests activities for you to do using Kid Pix. For example, you will read about totem poles in the Pacific Northwest and then follow steps to carve your own. The activities come from all around the world. Look at the map on pages 8 and 9. A picture from each activity shows the region from which the activity comes. To learn how to pronounce different words, look in the Glossary at the end of the book.

Each story is accompanied by drawings created with computer drawing programs for adults. Many of them are done in styles commonly found in that culture. All of the step-by-step activity drawings were created using Kid Pix on a color Macintosh computer. Don't worry if your Kid Pix program doesn't have the same colors or Rubber Stamps as the ones in this book. They are different for Macintosh, PC DOS, and PC Windows. Use the ones you find in your own program and see what you create! If you have a black and white printer, you can color your pictures with crayons.

Turn on your computer and Kid Pix and set up your printer with paper. Then try the Kid Pix Travel Kit activity. You may want to do these activities by yourself or with family or friends. Pack your bags and come travel around the world with Kid Pix. Have fun!

Your Kid Pix World Travel Guide,

Barbara J. Chan

ARCTIC OCEAN
ARCTIC
SIBERIA
ARCTIC
PACIFIC NORTHWEST
JAPAN
UNITED STATES
ATLANTIC
OCEAN
PACIFIC OCEAN
LATIN AMERICA
AUSTRALIA

ARCTIC OCEAN
SIBERIA
SWEDEN
UKRAINE
SWITZERLAND
GREECE
ITALY
CHINA
IRAN (Persia)
WEST AFRICA
GHANA
BENIN
INDIAN OCEAN
ATLANTIC OCEAN
N
AUSTRALIA

KID PIX TRAVEL KIT

Before you begin your trip around the world, check out your Kid Pix travel kit. You will use the many Kid Pix tools and features to learn about the people and places you visit.

1. Scribble with the Wacky Pencil. Click on it, press the mouse button down, and draw on your screen. Can you hear the scratchy noises as you draw? Click your mouse on the question mark at the bottom of your screen and draw again. What do you see?

2. Select different line widths from the boxes at the bottom of the screen. Draw more lines. Notice that the lines are thinner or thicker, depending on which width you choose.

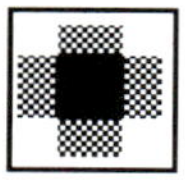

3. Select different Wacky Pencil effects by clicking on one of the boxes at the lower right. Draw a few more lines. Click on the Tint feature to get a watercolor effect. If you have a color screen, draw a magenta line and then draw a yellow line over it. The color turns to red. If your screen is black and white, draw a dark gray line and then draw a watercolor line over it. Experiment with other color combinations.

4. Uh oh! You don't like the colors? No problem. Click on the Undo Guy. He'll get rid of that last scribble.

5. Flip through the boxes at the bottom of the screen by clicking on the arrow at the lower right corner. Now draw with the round pencils.

6. Have some fun with the Wacky Brush. Click on the Brush and then click on the first box at the bottom of the screen. It's called the Leaky Pen. What happens when you paint with this brush that goes "Boolp boolp boolp" as you move it over your Kid Pix page? Press the Option or Ctrl key on your keyboard as you dribble your Leaky Pen all over the Kid Pix page.

7. If you painted something you don't want, use the Eraser to change it. Click on the Eraser. Experiment with the four shapes in the boxes at the bottom of the screen. Rub the ? Eraser all over your drawing. What happens to it?

8. Click on the Wacky Brush again. S-s-sp, S-s-sp, S-s-sp Spray Paint! If you have a color screen, choose a color. Now hold the Option or Ctrl key down while you spray and see what happens.

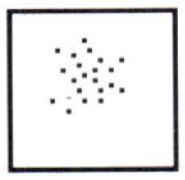

9. Do you want to get rid of the whole drawing? No big deal. The Eraser can do it. Click on the Stick Figure or the Firecracker and then click on your picture. Make another drawing and try the other options too.

10. Move part of your drawing from one place to another. Select the Moving Van and one of the boxes at the bottom of the screen. Click on a section of your drawing and drag it to another part of the screen. Whoa, slow down! Hear those screeching tires? Don't get a ticket traveling around the world with Kid Pix!

PAPER DESIGNS (Around the World)

Children everywhere love to play with paper. They paint, color, and print on it; fold, tear, crumple, and shred it; and cut, paste, and weave it. Over the years, the use of paper has spread throughout the world.

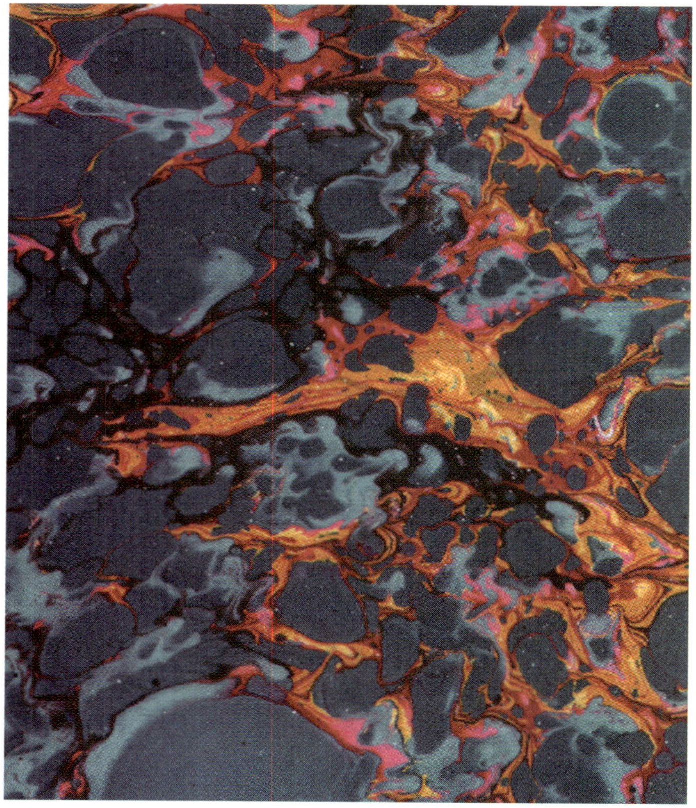

Did you know that paper was first made by pounding wet mulberry tree bark and small pieces of old fishing nets and silk and then hanging it on bamboo frames to dry? The Chinese first made paper that way by hand in the first century A.D. Eight hundred years later, papermakers made paper with hemp and flax fibers. Eventually, the secret of papermaking was taken to Europe. There, the Spanish invented a machine to grind the fibers into pulp. Papermakers in France, Germany, the Netherlands, and England used machines to make paper in the fifteenth century. Today hardly any paper is made by hand. Most of it is made using very big machines in factories called paper mills.

People were not content just to make paper. They wanted to decorate it too. The Persians floated different colors of oil paints on water, stirred it gently, and then laid paper on top of the mixture. The result was marbled paper, so-called because the paint patterns look like marble stone.

Design Your Own Paper

You can't mix oil paint and water with a computer, but with the Kid Pix tools you explored earlier you can design your own marbled paper.

1. 

Use the Wacky Pencil and the Question Mark to draw some wavy lines on the screen. Change the pencil width and change the shape from square to round. Choose different colors or patterns.

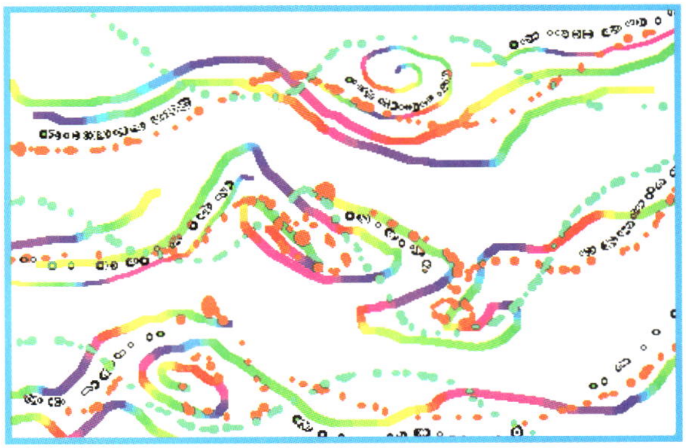

2. 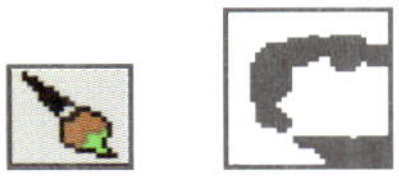

Dribble different colored inks with the Wacky Brush and Leaky Pen.

3. 

Use the Wacky Brush and the 3-D option to add some shaded lines.

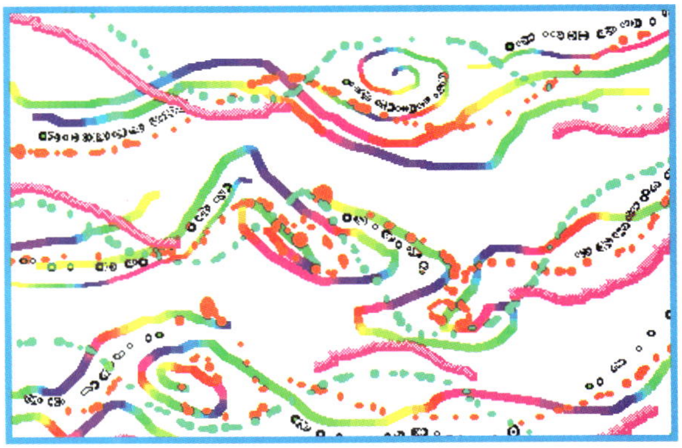

4. 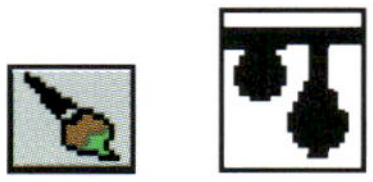

Now drip some Drippy Paint with the Wacky Brush.

5. 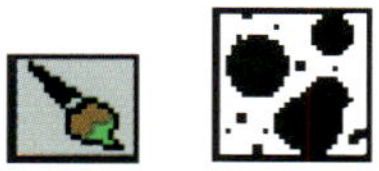

Splatter some paint with the Wacky Brush all over the painting.

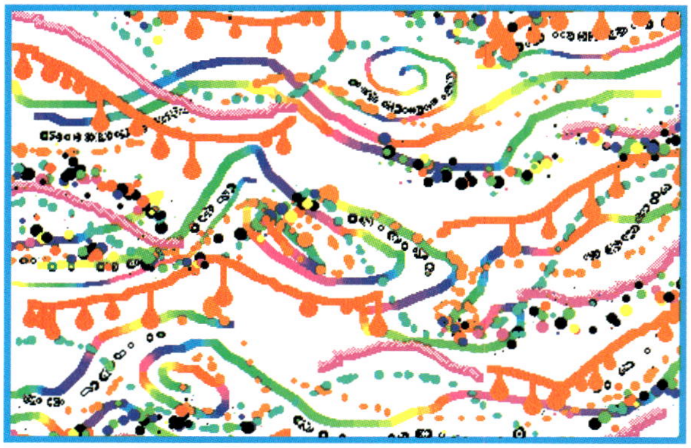

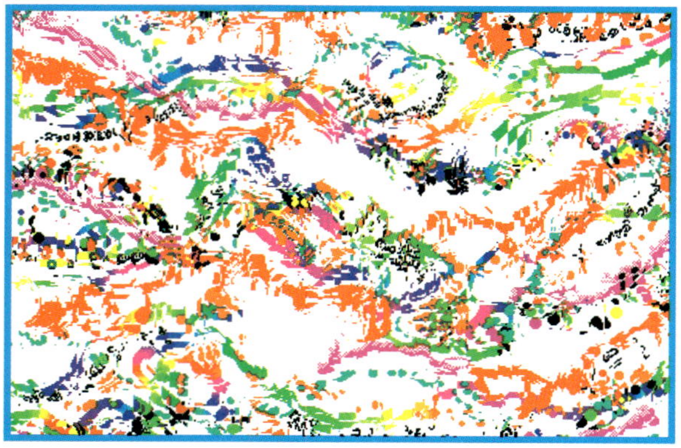

6. 

The Wacky Brush with the Fuzzer is just the right tool to mix up your Kid Pix paints. Move the Fuzzer back and forth all over your drawing to "stir" the colors.

7. 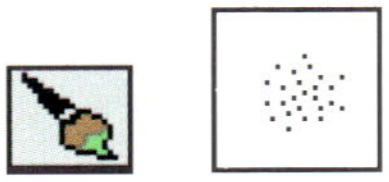

Marbled papers sometimes have flecks of gold color. Spritz some gold on your marbled paper with the Wacky Brush and Spray Paint.

Making Things With Paper

You can use your custom designed paper in many ways. You can wrap a present or make a small gift card with it. You can fold it into a box or, if you know Japanese paper folding called origami, you can fold it into a small animal or other shape. You can print several pages of your design and tape them together to make a larger piece. With this you can cover one of your books. You can make paper collage. Here is an example of marbled paper cut into circles which are pasted onto colored construction paper and used as a placemat.

PICTURE STORY (The Arctic)

Far north in the Arctic, which covers parts of northeastern Siberia, Alaska, Canada, and Greenland, live the Inuit whom many people called Eskimos. Before modern times Inuit, which means "The People" in their language, paddled large walrus-skinned boats called umiaks, searching the sea for salmon and trout.

When the Inuit came home with their catch, they told stories to their children about their adventures. The Inuit did not have a written language then. Some of them recorded their stories by painting pictures on wooden objects, such as their umiak paddles, or by carving them onto elkhorn spoons, bone knives, or pipes. Today, some young Inuit people are learning these traditional ways of recording their life histories from their elders.

This umiak paddle is like an old one found in northern Alaska. It shows how the Inuit recorded their stories with pictures of their adventures.

Record an Arctic Adventure

Kid Pix Rubber Stamps make it easy to record events. To see the stamp palette at the bottom of your screen, select the Rubber Stamp tool. Click your mouse in the palette boxes to select different stamps. When you click on the numbered arrow, you can see more stamps. There are eight different palettes, each with 14 different rubber stamps.

If you're using a Macintosh, press the Option, Shift, or Option + Shift keys when you stamp your picture. If you're using a PC, press the Ctrl, Shift, or Ctrl + Shift keys. The stamps get bigger and bigger.

Without using words, use just the stamps to record the following adventure about Inuits paddling their umiak on the ocean.

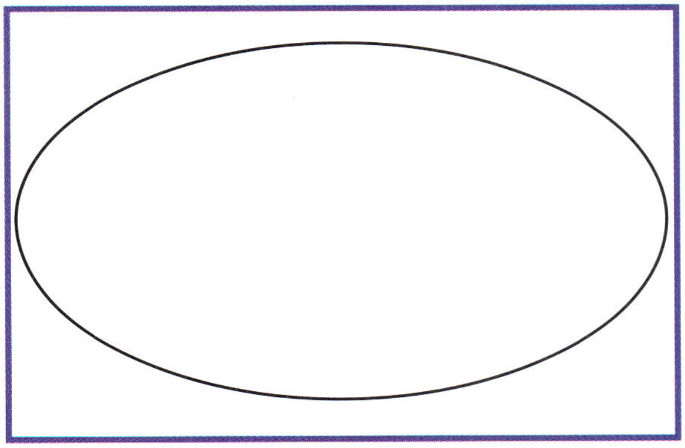

1. 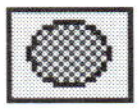

First, use the Oval to draw the blade of an umiak paddle.

2. 

As the Inuit began their journey, they spotted some sea birds. Find a bird stamp and click it on your paddle.

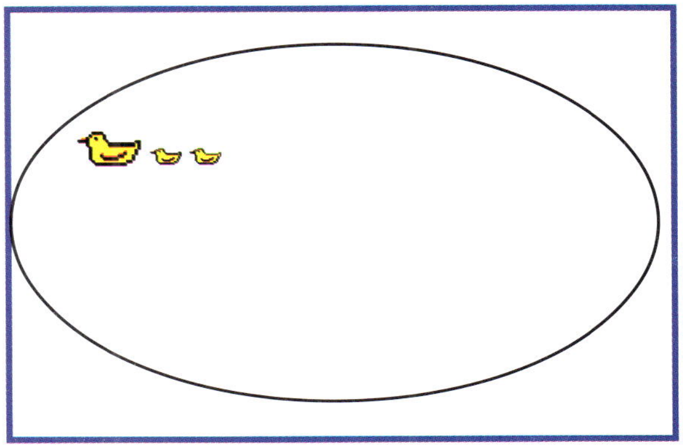

3.

Next the Inuits saw some small and big fish. Find some fish stamps and stamp big and small fish on your paddle.

4.

The Inuit traveled at night and could see the moon and stars.

5.

From their umiak the Inuit saw a bear on the shore in front of a tree.

6.

Although they were frightened, they had their trusty dog who barked and scared the bear away.

7.

The Inuit had been fishing all night. Soon it would be morning. They decided to paddle back home. On the way they saw some small rabbits on the shore.

Record Your Own Adventure

Now that you know how the Inuit recorded their adventures, think of an object like a baseball bat, soccer ball, or car that is important to you or your culture and draw it on your screen. Then use Kid Pix Rubber Stamps to record one of your own stories. Print out your story and share it with a friend. Find out if they can "read" and understand your adventures.

PATCHWORK QUILTS (United States)

Log cabin, windmill, Star of Bethlehem, feather, garden basket, honeycomb, and crazy are just some of the many names given to patchwork patterns. Quilters have been making these bed coverlets from the time pioneers first came to the land that is now called the United States. Now, as then, they follow the same steps to make these traditional quilts.

Quilt makers cut shapes from scraps of colored cloth and sew them by hand into squares or other shapes. Quilt designs depend on the shapes that are used. Rectangles, triangles, diamonds, stars, fruit, flowers, leaves, or birds are sewn together to make a "patch."

After they make the patches, quilt makers sew them together to make one large rectangle. They sew shapes together to make a border around the patches. Altogether, this is called the quilt cover.

To make the quilt, they sew together the cover, a layer of warm cotton or wool, and a large piece of cloth as the backing. To finish the coverlet, they sew tiny running stitches in special quilting designs. These designs might be flowers, stems and leaves, birds or other animals, hearts or circles, straight or curved lines. The finished quilt often becomes a treasured family heirloom.

Design a Crazy Quilt Patch

The crazy quilt wasn't really crazy. It was made from odd shapes of silk and velvet cloth, often left over from making clothing or recycled from worn clothes. The pieces were sewn as patches and decorated with fancy embroidery stitches. The embroidery became an important part of the overall design.

With the Kid Pix Rectangle and shapes filled with patterns you can make a wonderful crazy quilt.

1. 

Draw a large white square. Select the Rectangle tool and click on the first box in the Options bar at the bottom of the screen. Hold the Shift key down as you drag the Rectangle across your screen.

2.

Using the Rectangle, place pieces of patterned "cloth" on your square. Click on one of the patterns at the bottom of the screen. Then select a color for each patch. Draw two or three filled rectangles inside the square.

3.

Add other bits of cloth. Select other colors and other patterns. Draw more rectangles inside the square. Make them overlap one another a little bit. Hold the Option or Ctrl key down as you draw. Does the border around the rectangle disappear?

4. 

You can cover the entire square with patterned rectangles of different colors. Now add some Kid Pix craziness to your quilt. Click on the Question mark and draw small rectangles to fill in the last white spaces. Here's a crazy quilt with rainbows!

5.  

Now do your embroidery stitches around the crazy pieces. With the Wacky Brush and Zig Zag, "stitch" the shapes together. Use different colors and draw your stitches around the edges of each section.

6. 

To make your crazy quilt extra special, use Rubber Stamps to embroider some fancy designs. Stamp flowers or animals on some of the shapes to make this your personal crazy quilt.

Make a Kid Pix Crazy Quilt

Now that you have made a patchwork quilt on the screen, make a paper Kid Pix crazy quilt. Design four different crazy quilt squares. Save and print each drawing. Use scissors to cut out the squares all the same size. Lay out a large piece of construction, butcher, or newsprint paper. Place two crazy quilt squares side by side on the large paper. This is one row. Place two other squares below the first row to make a second row. Glue the squares down to finish your crazy quilt.

KINGLIST CLOTH (Benin)

Have you ever seen a story-telling banner or umbrella? If you visit Benin, a small country on Africa's Gold Coast, you might see one with figures of people, animals, or weapons. These figures are cut from colorful fabric and stitched by hand onto large cloths by a method called appliqué. Until the late 1800s, only kings belonging to the Fon court used these kinglist cloths to display their wealth and power. A typical cloth showed conquests or hunting or fishing scenes. Others depicted a large king with smaller citizens around him.

A kinglist cloth had symbols describing the many names that the king had. The king used to say all his names in long sentences when he spoke at different events. Every name sentence used specific words and phrases to identify the king and explain his hopes and victories.

Gangnihessou, the first Fon king's name, means chief (gan) is (gni) male bird (hessou). When he passed his people, they would chant his name sentence: "The chief is a great male bird who dominates all the world so that one must announce him everywhere with the beating of the drum." His emblems were the vulture and a drum. Another Fon king, King Agonglo, had a name that means pineapple (agon) and impossible (glo). According to one legend, Agonglo held onto a pineapple plant when his enemies attacked him with lightning.

After the last Fon king died, the tailors guild began making kinglist cloths for other people. Although they are still very colorful, the scenes shown on the newer hangings have changed with the times and show less violence. The lion even smiles!

Create a Kinglist Cloth

Paint a kinglist cloth about an imaginary king whose name means "pineapple male bird" (Agonhessou). Tell the story of his trip on a ship to catch a big fish.

1.  

Use the Wacky Pencil and yellow to draw the outline of a pineapple. Make it large and bold. Use the Paint Can and the same yellow color to fill the outline.

2. 

Draw the ridges on the pineapple. Draw the leaves at the top.

3.

Use the Wacky Pencil and Paint Can to draw the vulture. You can draw the eye with the Oval.

4.

Use the Wacky Pencil to draw the ship and its mast.

Use the Oval to draw one porthole. Now copy and paste that oval to make two more portholes. Select the Moving Van and the Magnet. Hold the mouse button down and drag the mouse across the oval from the upper left to the lower right. A blinking box will appear. Select Copy from the Edit menu. Now select Paste from the Edit menu and move the hole next to the first one. Click the mouse button to paste down the second hole. Repeat this step to put in more portholes.

Use the Line to draw horizontal lines across the outside of the ship.

5. 

Add some fish to your drawing. Draw some with the Wacky Pencil or put some in with the Rubber Stamp.

6. 

After you have finished drawing the symbols, use the Paint Can and black to fill in the cloth.

Make Your Own Kinglist Cloth

Now that you know about the Fon kings and their kinglist cloths, imagine having your own name sentence that people chant as you pass by. What would your name and that sentence be? Draw a cloth to show them. Make a drawing with pictures or symbols to represent three important events that have occurred in your lifetime. You may also want to make a personal history drawing with pictures that represent your own experiences. Print these drawings out and share them with your friends. See if they can identify the symbols with you.

WINTER (Switzerland)

How would you like to climb the famous Matterhorn, a mountain that is more than 14,000 feet (4,300 meters) high? It is part of the Swiss Alps, a range of mountains that stretches across Switzerland. The word "alp" probably comes from the Latin word "alb," which means white or the color of snow. In late fall and winter, deep snow covers the Alps. Even in summer, you can see snow on the tallest peaks.

Like children in other snowy places, Swiss kids play outside after school making snow men and women, tossing snowballs, sledding, and skiing. Many Swiss children grow up learning to ski. Some even ski between home and school.

Families who live in towns near the Matterhorn can take a train to the ski slopes. When they arrive near the bottom of the big mountain, they get off the train. Everyone puts on woolen caps, warm waterproof jackets, and mittens. They strap on skis before heading up the slopes. The best thing about skiing around the Matterhorn is that when the skiers get cold or tired, they can stop in a small hut and drink a cup of hot chocolate!

Discover a Winter Scene with Kid Pix

1.

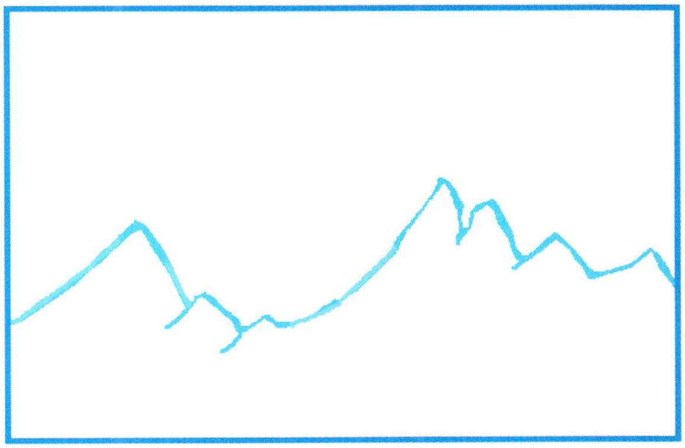

When you are standing on the Matterhorn, there are mountains all around you. Use the Wacky Pencil and a sky color to draw a wavy line of mountains from edge to edge. Include a high peak like the Matterhorn.

2.

With the Paint Can fill the sky with color. Did you hear the paint pour out of the Can when you clicked your mouse?

3.

Trees grow in the Alps. Place some trees near the bottom of the mountains. Look through the Rubber Stamp palettes and choose a tree you like. Make different-sized trees by holding down the Option, Shift, or Option + Shift keys on a Macintosh when you stamp your picture. If you're using a PC, press the Ctrl, Shift, or Ctrl + Shift keys.

4. 

Show the train you rode to get to the Matterhorn. Find the train cars among the Rubber Stamps and place a small train near the bottom of your drawing.

5. 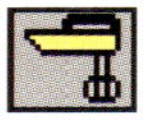 

Wow, it just started to snow! See what happens when you choose the Electric Mixer and the Snow Flakes and Rain Drops feature. Click your mouse around the screen and watch the snowflakes fall!

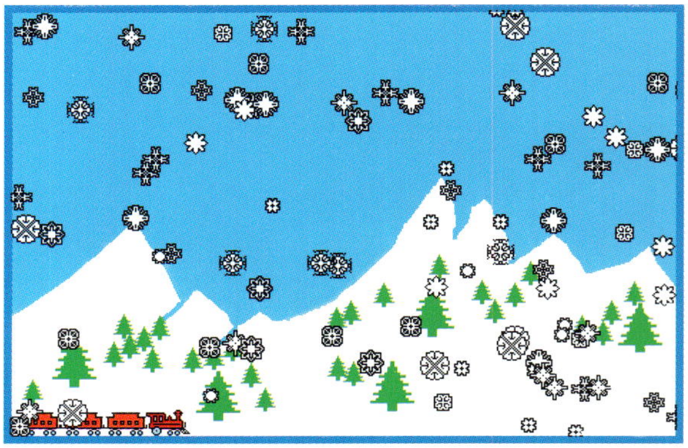

6.  

Look at the snowflakes close up by clicking your mouse on the Zoom In pattern. Now click on the center of one of the snowflakes. Click it again and again. Notice that the snowflake gets bigger and bigger until you can only see one or two giant snowflakes on your screen.

7.

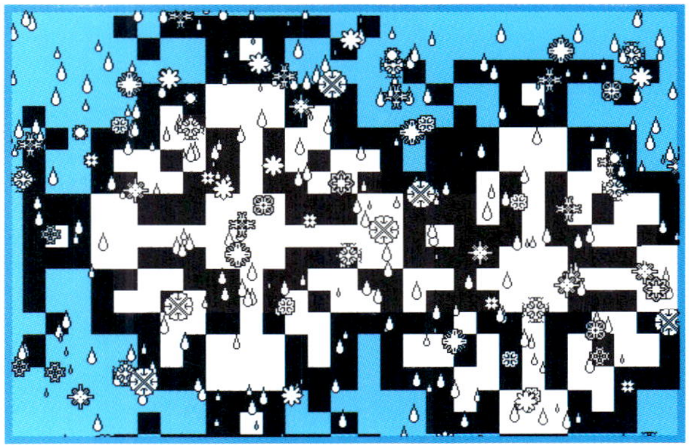

It's beginning to rain. Hold down the Option or Ctrl key and click on the Snow Flakes and Rain Drops feature again. Move the cursor onto the screen, hold your mouse button down, and watch the rain fall. Try pressing the Option or Ctrl key and releasing it several times. It rains, then snows, then rains again—just like in the mountains!

Paint Your Own Winter Scene

Paint a winter scene. Even if you have never been in a place with snow, draw an imaginary picture with snow, mountains, and trees. Draw a picture of yourself playing in the snow. Would you build a snowman? What is winter like where you live? Draw a picture of your own winter fun.

KAMON (Japan)

Long ago, Japanese samurai warriors wore kamon embroidered on their clothes and painted on their possessions. Kamon are family crests—designs with plants, animals, or other symbols often placed inside a circle or square. Each Japanese family has a kamon.

Today, traditional Japanese clothing is often embroidered with kamon and worn for special occasions such as baby parties, weddings, or festivals. Men, women, and children wear kimonos, which are full-length silk robes, and haoris, which are jackets.

When a young woman gets married, her family may have a small silk scarf, called a fukusa, printed with their kamon. They wrap a wedding gift inside the fukusa and give it to their daughter. Some families have a lacquer bowl and tray set embossed with their kamon and give it to their baby when it is thirty days old.

From its beginnings in ancient Japan with samurai warriors, the kamon continues today as an important symbol of each Japanese family's heritage.

Design a Kamon

Imagine that it is your job to design a kamon for a samurai warrior. Here are some suggestions for designing one in a circle.

1. 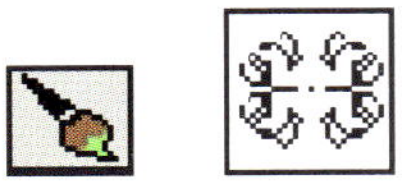

Make a loop pattern for the central part of your design. Use the Wacky Brush and Caterpillars. Click on the arrow at the bottom of your screen to get to the second palette and find Caterpillars. Hold down the mouse button and move your Brush around on the screen until you like the pattern.

2. 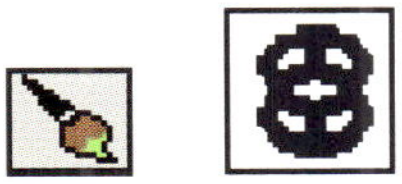

Use the Wacky Brush and Kaleidoscope to draw another pattern over the Caterpillars. You will find Kaleidoscope by clicking on the arrow to see the other palette. Choose another color or shade of gray for this pattern.

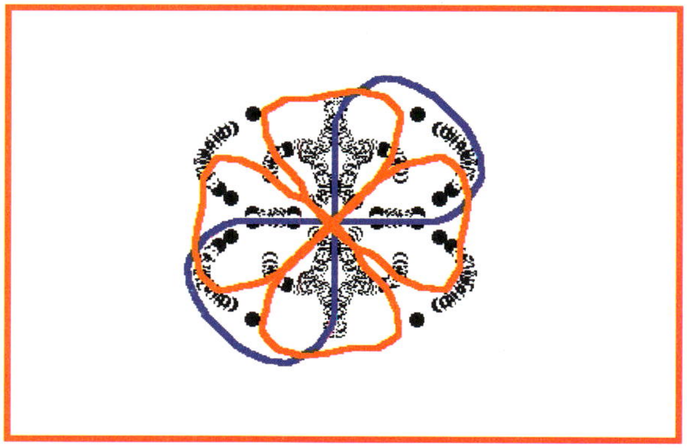

3.

Now draw another shape going in the other direction.

4.

Draw a large circle around your design. Select the Oval tool and click on the first box in the Options bar at the bottom of your screen. If you want a perfect circle, hold down the Shift key while you use the mouse to draw. If the circle is not exactly where you want it, click the Undo Guy and try again.

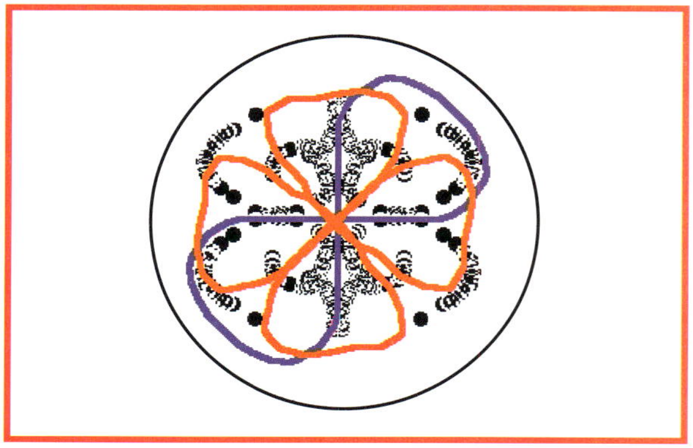

There! You have created a kamon. You may want to save the drawing. Follow the directions for saving drawings in the “Around the World Toolkit” section on page 6.

Design Your Own Kamon

Now that you know something about family crests in Japan, use Kid Pix to create a kamon for your own family.

Perhaps you have a favorite animal or like the way a certain flower looks. Maybe you want to make a special design that is yours alone. Explore Kid Pix tools and use them to create your very own kamon. After you have designed your family crest, you can put it on your clothes. Here's how to do it.

1. Print your kamon.
2. Glue it onto a piece of thin cardboard to make it stiff.
3. Use a pair of scissors to cut out the kamon.
4. Pin the kamon to your clothing or ask an adult to help you. When friends ask you what it is, you can tell them about Japanese kamon and how you made your own personal one with Kid Pix.

TIGER SLIPPERS (China)

How would you like a tiger to protect you? This big cat was very important in China during the years known as the Ming dynasty. From 1368 to 1644 people hung pictures of the tiger on the wall on the Lixia holiday, which happened on the fifth day of the fifth month each year. They believed that the tiger had magic powers to keep them healthy and safe. Some Chinese people wore tiger claws to prevent illness. Others made medicine with the tiger's bones and ashes.

Chinese people thought sons were the most precious members of any family. Mothers in the countryside often sewed hats, bibs, collars, and slippers in the shape of a tiger to keep their baby sons from harm. They gave them these clothes when their sons were thirty days or one hundred days old. The mothers used beautiful stitches and padded shapes of colorful cloth to create the three-dimensional ears, nose, mouth, and eyes. Some made their tigers look very real; others stitched fantasy versions. Some mothers even made pillows with two tiger heads to protect their sons while they were sleeping.

When Chinese mothers made slippers, they padded the soles with layers of paper and cloth to make the slippers soft for their children to walk in. They sewed tiger faces onto the front of the slippers. When the children walked, everyone could see the tigers coming.

Today in modern China, some mothers continue the tradition of making tiger clothing for their children. Unlike their ancestors, these Chinese moms make colorful tiger clothes for both their sons and daughters.

Draw a Tiger Slipper

You can design some tiger slippers with Kid Pix.

1.

Tiger slippers are often shaped like moccasins. Draw the shape of your slipper with the Wacky Pencil and one of your favorite colors or shades of gray. Use a yellow Wacky Pencil to draw the tiger head. Pour yellow paint into the head with the Paint Can. Draw two smaller yellow circles with the filled Oval for the ears.

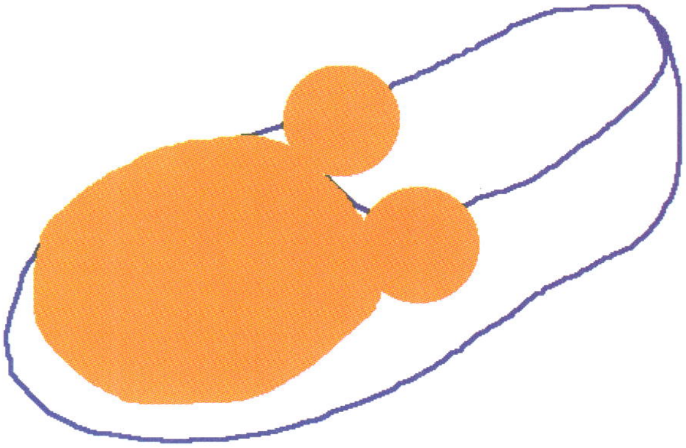

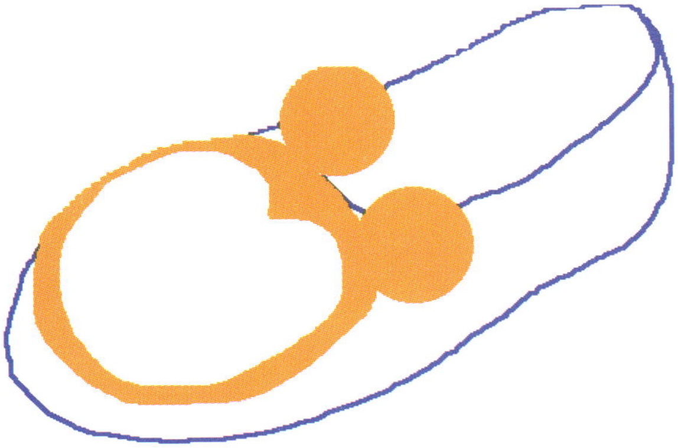

2.

Now draw the tiger's white face. Use a white Wacky Pencil to draw the outline and then pour white paint into the face with the Paint Can.

If you are using a black-and-white monitor, use the Eraser to erase the inside of the tiger's face to make it white.

3. 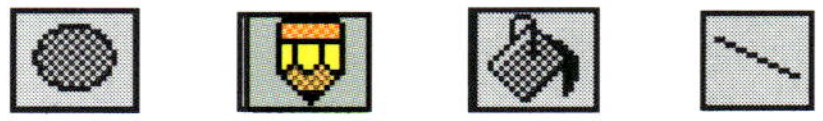

Next, draw the tiger's eyes with the filled Oval using black. Draw the nose with the Wacky Pencil and use the Paint Can to fill it in. Use the Wacky Pencil to draw the eyebrows and mouth. The Line tool makes great whiskers.

4. 

With a thin Wacky Pencil, sketch in the long hair that tigers have around their whole face and ears. In the Chinese mountainside, the tiger often has white or pale yellow hair.

5. 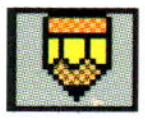

With a thicker black Wacky Pencil, draw the tiger's face stripes.

6. 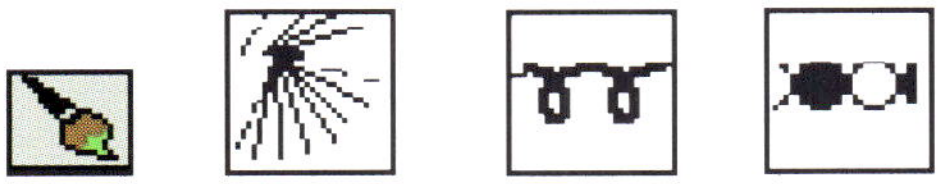

Chinese mothers use colored thread to embroider beautiful stitches on the slippers. The Kid Pix Wacky Brush with Swirl, Looper, or Dots makes a great embroidery tool. Use Swirl and a flower color to draw some spiky flowers along the side of your slipper. With other colors, draw loops and dots around the toes and the opening of the slippers. Your slipper will look almost like the one my Chinese great grandmother made for my grandfather a long time ago.

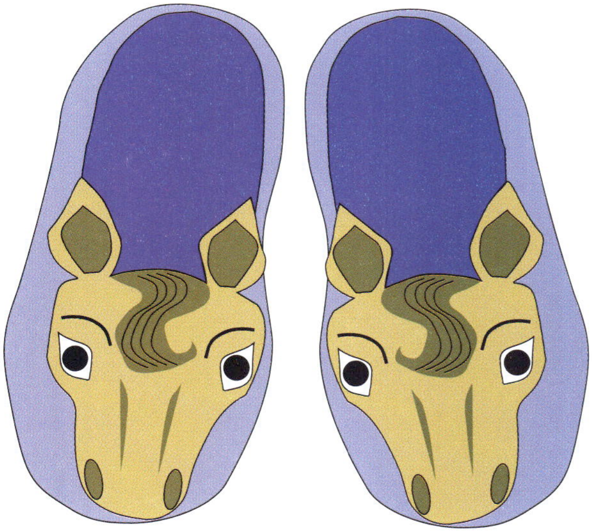

Design Your Own Animal Slipper

Maybe you have a favorite animal whom you feel gives you protection. Use Kid Pix to draw your animal. Print two copies, cut them out and pin them to your slippers or shoes. Isn't it fun to have your own slippers inspired by Chinese mothers and children?

PAINTED WALLS (West Africa)

Think about living in a house decorated all over with patterns and symbols. In some parts of West Africa women have been decorating their houses with colored paint for many generations. Each year after the rainy season they paint new designs on their walls to celebrate festive occasions such as a marriage or birth.

Women in each community get together and choose colors to decorate their homes. Only women who have learned wall painting from their mothers may paint the buildings. Women who are not trained as painters gather the materials and mix the colors. They grind leaves and red, black, and ochre soil to make green, red, black, and yellow paints.

Painters are often accompanied by children playing around them and by babies tucked onto their backs. They paint beautiful geometric or abstract patterns on their mud-walled houses. The designs include plants (like the calabash squash) or animals (like an insect or lizard) found commonly in their community. Sometimes, a painter draws a scorpion on the wall to warn children not to play with this

dangerous insect. In some regions, designers make mud animals in three-dimensional relief and then paint them. Igbo women in Nigeria sometimes paint symbols showing war scenes or their roles in the family.

Some West African women use white chalk to represent happiness and success. Others use white for purity. Some use red when a person dies; others use red to brighten their designs. Usually the women paint with their hands and fingers. Sometimes they use sticks, leaves, or stones to apply the colors.

Traditionally, girls watch, help, and learn how to do wall painting from their mothers. Boys also grow up around painting mothers, and the lives of everyone in the community are brightened by the colorful patterns they see around them. Today in West Africa the painters continue to pass on their wall decoration customs to the younger generation.

Build a West African House

Typical painted West African homes have mud walls and a thatched roof. Some have curved walls and round doorways. Kid Pix painting tools are ideal for designing and decorating a house like those found in West Africa.

1. 

Use the Rectangle filled with mud color to draw the basic shape. As you draw your rectangle, think about this question: Is your house wide or tall?

2.

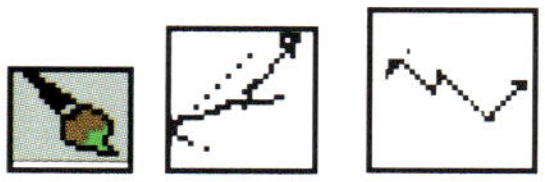

Now put a straw roof on your rectangle to make it look like a house. Straw is thin and yellow or golden brown. There are several Kid Pix tools that work well for painting straw. Use the Wacky Brush with the Pine Needles. Hold down the Option or Ctrl key when drawing with Pine Needles to make them thicker. You can also use the Wacky Brush and Zig Zag.

3.

The Wacky Pencil, Oval, and Paint Can are great for designing a walkway wall or a food storage room in front of the house.

4.

You can draw two shapes to make an arched doorway. First draw a filled Oval for the top of the doorway. Then draw a tall filled Rectangle that overlaps the bottom of the oval.

5. 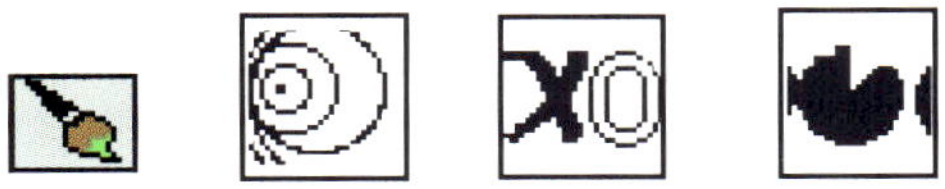

Now that you have built your house, what decorations do you want to paint on the walls? There are many Kid Pix tools from which to choose. Use some of the tools you have used in other activities, or try ones you haven't used before. Try using the Wacky Brush and Echoes, Hugs and X's, and Pies. Go ahead, be wild! If you don't like your wall painting design, just Undo or Erase it and try again.

Design Your Own Painted House

If you could have your own painted house, how would it look? Would it have more than one floor? Would it have mud walls like those in West Africa? Use Kid Pix to design your own imaginary house.

CANCIONES (Latin America)

People everywhere love songs. Settlers brought canciones, which is Spanish for songs, from Spain when they came to Central America, the Greater Antilles, and South America several hundred years ago.

In this part of the world, mothers and fathers sing songs about places, people, and events to their babies and young children. Walking to school, you might hear a mother crooning a song to her child about a lovely pájaro (bird) making its nest. In the evening, you might hear a father counting elefantes (elephants) in a song with his children. You might hear school kids from Puerto Rico to Mexico and from Venezuela to Argentina singing different versions of the same song. Scenes, customs, and vocabulary of each area become part of the songs, and each region may have different words for describing them. For example, in Puerto Rico people call a bird pájaro and in Argentina they may call it pájara. If you travel in Spanish-speaking Latin America, you may hear pájaros or pájaras sing their own canciones.

Write a Song and Learn Sounds

Kid Pix makes it easy to write a song and learn sounds of the alphabet. Here is a Spanish language song from Puerto Rico with its English translation.

¡Qué linda manito!

Qué linda manito
que tiene el bebé
qué linda, qué mona,
qué bonita es.
Pequeños deditos
rayitos de sol,
que gire que gire
como un girasol

A Pretty Little Hand

How pretty, how little,
This sweet baby's hand.
So soft—Oh! So pretty!
How lovely it is.
Fingers so tiny
Like small rays of sun.
Around and around
Like a twinkling sunflower

You may notice that, although the same letters are used to write English and Spanish, some letters in Spanish have marks above them. The letters have different names and are pronounced differently in each language.

Write two or three lines of the song which you would like to illustrate.

1. 

Select the Text tool to stamp the words in Spanish. Then select Switch to Spanish from the Goodies menu. Notice the Spanish words at the top of the screen. Archivo means File. Edición means Edit. Delicias means Goodies. Kid Pix on a Macintosh pronounce each letter in Spanish when you click the letters. Choose letters from the boxes at the bottom of your screen. Click on the arrow to see more letters and numbers.

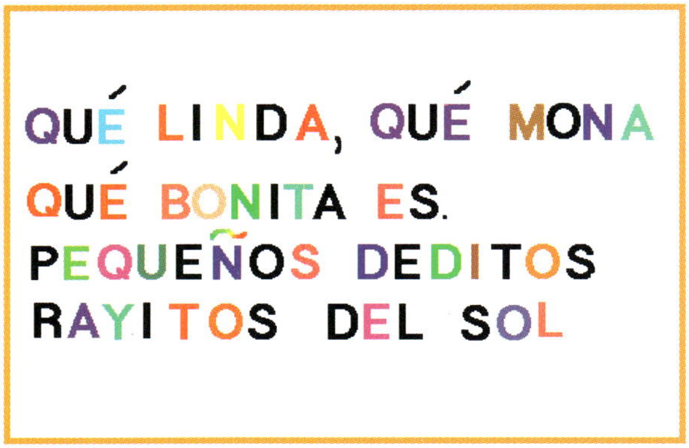

2. 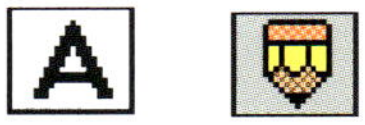

If you have a color screen, you can stamp the letters in different colors. Click your mouse on the color, then select the letter, and stamp it on the screen. Stamp the rest of the letters from the words in the song. Kid Pix does not have a period, so draw it with the Wacky Pencil. You will also have to draw the accent mark above the E as in *qué* and the tilde above the N as in *pequeño.*

Type the Song

You can also type letters with the Kid Pix Text tool.

1. 

Select Cambiar al Inglés from the Delicias menu. The menus change to English. To type the English version of the lines from the song, press the Option or Ctrl key down, then click your mouse on the Text tool. The alphabet at the bottom of your screen changes to a row of eight As. There are eight different styles of letters to choose from. Release the Option or Ctrl key, then click on the type style you want to use. Click your mouse on the screen where you want to begin typing and type the words from the song in English. Press the Return key after you type the last word in each line. The cursor moves to the next line.

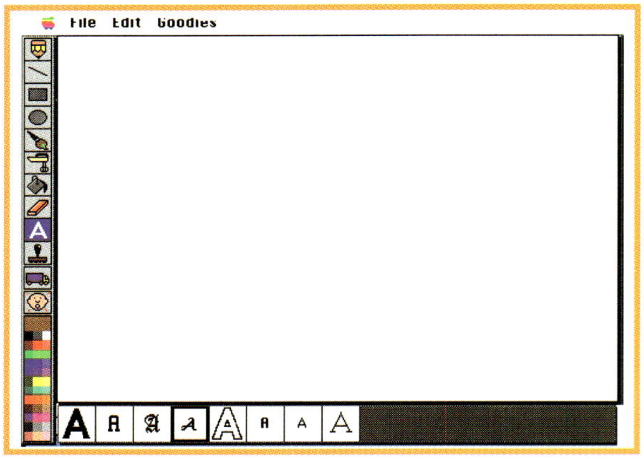

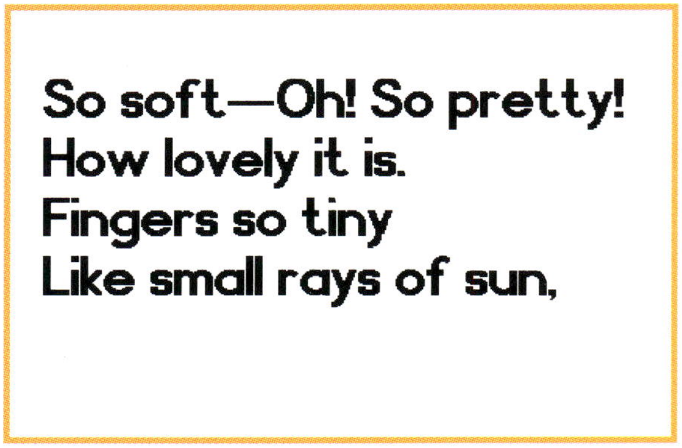

Illustrate Your Song

Use the Kid Pix tools to draw pictures to illustrate the song.

1. 

Use Wacky Pencil, Wacky Brush, and Rubber Stamps to draw pictures to accompany the song in English and Spanish. How about a sunflower or baby?

Record a Song

If your computer has a microphone, you can record sounds and songs to go with your drawings using Macintosh and Windows versions of Kid Pix.

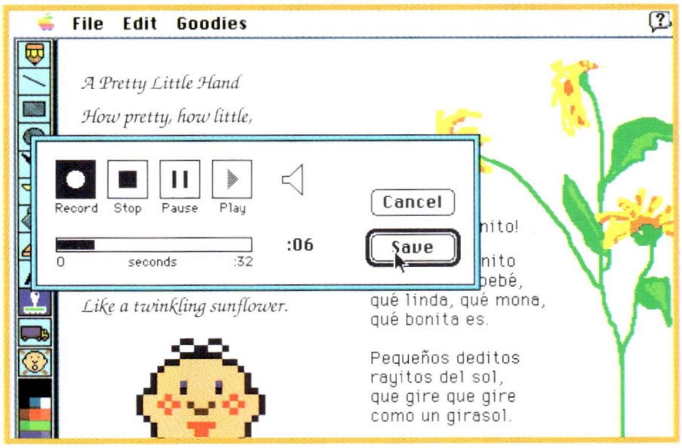

1. Make up a tune to go with the lines you have written from "Qué linda manito." Select Record a Sound from the Goodies menu. Click the Record button in the dialog box that appears on your screen and sing your song while Kid Pix records it. Click the Stop button when you are finished.

Click on the Play button to hear your recording. If you want to change it, you can record it again or record a new song. You can also record music from a record, cassette tape, compact disc, or even from the radio.

Click on the Save button. Whenever you want to hear the song while the drawing is open, select Play Sound from the Goodies menu.

Try recording and playing other songs.

VALENTINES (United States)

Red hearts pierced with arrows, pink hearts pasted onto white lace doilies, and cherubs shooting arrows say, "Be mine, Valentine!" Every year on February 14 people in the United States make Valentine's Day cards to send to people they love: mothers, fathers, sisters, brothers, grandmothers, grandfathers, aunts, uncles, teachers, and friends.

People began celebrating Valentine's Day in Europe hundreds of years ago. The custom became popular in the United States during the 1700s. Young men often proposed marriage to their sweethearts by sending them a True Love Knot valentine. The Love Knot was made of cutout heart shapes with messages that had no beginning or end. Girl friends responded by sending homemade valentines. People enjoyed making cards painted with houses, trees, men, and women with part of the design pricked out with pins and needles and notes decorated with lace, bits of ribbon, and flowers.

American children today make and decorate bright, beautiful Valentine's Day cards. Some even use their computers to make valentines! Some cards are formal with lace and hearts and some are humorous with modern cartoon characters and jokes. No matter how kids design them, valentine cards all carry the same message—"I love you."

A Modern Valentine

Kid Pix has wonderful features to help you make a valentine for someone special. Many lace valentines are made with paper doilies, which are circles of white paper with cutouts of flowers, animals, or shapes. Kids paste red or pink paper hearts on them and sometimes decorate them with sequins, glitter, or ribbons.

1. 

To begin designing your doily, first draw a large gray or blue Rectangle on your screen. The lace you paint on it will show up better on this background.

Use the Wacky Brush and the Geometry pattern to paint large, lacy patterns on the background so they make a "doily." If you are using a color computer, select white color. When you hold the mouse button down as you paint, you will get the same pattern over and over. When you click the mouse and paint again, a new Geometry pattern will appear.

2. 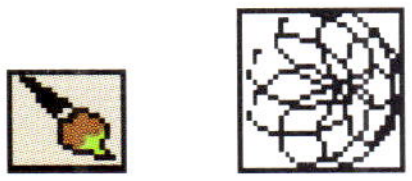

Select another color and click your mouse in the center of your doily. Hold the Option or Ctrl key down, then press the mouse button to paint Geometry. The pattern gets larger. If you like, paint the large pattern one or two more times to make it stand out better.

3. 

Now Rubber Stamp a giant red heart in the middle of your doily. Pressing the Option + Shift or Ctrl + Shift keys makes the stamp very big. If you don't like the shiny white spots on the heart, use the Paint Can to fill them with red paint. Cover some of the black jagged edges on the heart by coloring over them with the Wacky Pencil and red.

4. 

"Roses are red, violets are blue, sugar is sweet, and so are you" is a popular valentine poem. Add some roses to your valentine with the Rubber Stamp. Try stamping them medium size by pressing the Option or Ctrl key as you click your mouse.

5. 

Now type your message. Hold the Option or Ctrl key down and click your mouse on the Text tool. Release the key and use your mouse to select a fancy letter style. Click the mouse on the valentine where you want your message to begin. You will see a blinking line. Type your message. If you want it to appear on two lines, press the Return key before typing the second line.

6.

If you're using a color computer, try giving your valentine a high tech look. Select the Paint Can and the Question Mark. Pour paint into the gray rectangle. Wow! Pour white paint into the Geometry patterns of the doily.

7.

If you want to really jazz up your valentine, experiment with the Electric Mixer. Be daring and use Checkerboard or the Highlighter for different special effects.

Create Your Own Valentine

Now that you know something about the history of valentines, design your own for someone special. Use any of the Kid Pix tools that you explored before. Then print the valentine out on white or colored paper. If you like, add some glitter or ribbon, sign your name, and present it to your loved one. Happy Valentine's Day!

TOTEM POLES (Pacific Northwest)

How would you feel if a big bear, a raven, and an Orca killer whale stared down at you from a cedar pole standing eighty feet high? If you were a Pacific Northwest Indian living along the coast in Alaska, British Columbia, or Washington, you might carve such totem poles ranging from five to eighty feet tall. For many generations, Tlingit, Tsimshian, Kwakiutl, Haida, and other tribes have carved these poles from cedar logs.

Animals and other figures are etched into these poles. Each figure and animal is significant. An old Tlingit pole had the owner's sea lion crest carved on the top. A raven in the middle represented his tribe. On the bottom was a frog, which symbolized some of his tribe's history.

According to a legend, a Tlingit woman insulted a frog and the Frog People took her to be punished. After her people rescued her, she couldn't eat any food and she died. The Tlingit believed that the Frog People caused her death because they were so powerful, so the Tlingit used the frog as a crest to protect themselves from further harm.

Some totem poles were erected near the center of the village. Others were placed in front of a person's home. During special ceremonies, people entered through a large hole carved near the bottom of the pole. Other poles were used to hold the ashes of Indians who had died. Now most of the poles have fallen and are lying on the ground, but a few are in museums.

Nowadays, Pacific Northwest elders teach younger members of the community how to carve totem poles to record and remember their history.

Create a Pacific Northwest Indian Totem Pole

You can use Kid Pix tools to carve a totem pole.

1. 

The carver finds a tall cedar tree, cuts it down, and removes all the bark. Use the Rectangle and a wood color to draw a tall filled rectangle. This will be your pole.

2.  

Next, decide which figures you want to carve into your pole. Draw animals and people with the Wacky Pencil or use Rubber Stamps. Draw or stamp the figures one above the other on the cedar pole.

3. 

Pacific Northwest Indians used chisels to carve their poles; you can use the Kid Pix Eraser to carve yours. Select the Eraser and one of the four shapes in the Options palette at the bottom of your screen. “Carve” the wood away from the figures you drew or stamped on the pole. If you accidentally erase too much of your drawing, immediately click the Undo Guy to get your drawing back.

Use the smallest eraser to carve the remaining wood away from your figures.

4. 

If your pole is to be used as a ceremonial entrance, carve a hole near the bottom. With the Oval and white color selected, draw an oval near the bottom of your pole. If your circle isn’t white, click the Undo Guy and try again.

Design and Build Your Own Totem Pole

Design a totem pole that means something to you and your extended family. Choose animals to represent your immediate family, your extended family, and yourself. Recall important experiences that people in your family have had and decide which animal or figure will represent each event.

Materials

round cereal box
printer
paper
scissors
tape

1. Use any of the Kid Pix tools you have learned about to draw or stamp the different animals or figures on your totem pole. You will need to draw your totem pole in two parts to fit on the cereal box. Draw the top half of the pole on the first painting. Print it. Draw the bottom half on the second painting and print it.
2. Line up the two drawings with the figures one above the other. Turn the pages over and apply tape on the back to tape the drawings together. Cut off the ends to fit the box if they are too long. Wrap the drawings around the cereal box and tape them to the box.
3. If any of your figures have wings, arms, legs, or beaks that extend beyond your finished drawings, draw them with Kid Pix now. Print them and use scissors to cut them out. Tape them where they belong on your totem pole. Now you have your own totem!

PYSANKY (Ukraine)

Have you ever seen a "written" egg? If you visit Ukraine in spring, you may see pysanky which are decorated by "writing" designs on them with melted beeswax and coloring them with yellow, blue, red, and black dyes. These special eggs get their name from the Ukrainian word pysaty, which means to write.

Eggs symbolize spring and rebirth to Ukrainians. Every Easter women make two kinds of decorated eggs. They hardboil and color some called krashanky and eat them later. They make pysanky from hollow eggs and give them away to family and friends.

To write on the egg, the artist uses a kistka, a tiny funnel on a handle, to drip the wax. She then dips the egg into yellow dye. All parts of the egg that are not covered by wax turn yellow. After drawing other designs on the egg with more melted wax, she dips the egg into another color, repeating this process until the design is complete. The final color in the series is usually black or red. Next, she warms the egg so the wax melts, then wipes it off, revealing the colorful patterns with white lines. Finally, she paints the egg with lacquer to keep it strong.

Ukrainians believed pysanky had special powers to heal the sick, ensure a good harvest, protect their homes from fire, and help couples have children. Today Ukrainians continue the tradition of exchanging pysanky with loved ones at Easter time. Mothers teach their daughters how to decorate the eggs. Although each egg is decorated differently, all have wide bands, triangles, or ovals in which the traditional symbols are painted. Eggs can be decorated with flowers and given to a fiancé. Pysanky painted with a chicken may be given to newlyweds. Whatever the design, sharing pysanky means sharing love.

Color a Pysanky Egg

With Kid Pix tools, you can draw and decorate your own pysanky. Here's how.

1. 

With the Oval, draw a very big egg on your screen. You can't paint white "wax" on a white Kid Pix egg, so paint the colored patterns on first. Draw two thick black lines across the egg with the Wacky Pencil. You may have to draw several lines next to each other to make them fit inside the oval.

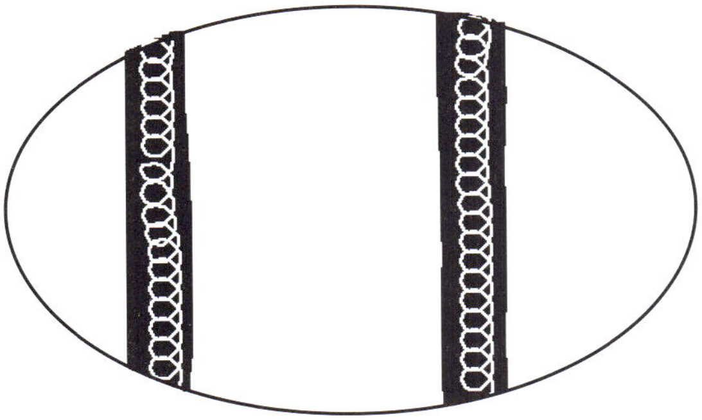

2. 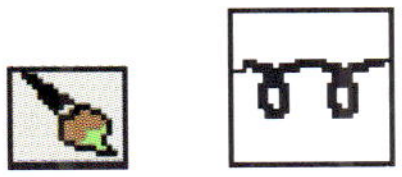

If you have a color screen, use the Wacky Brush and the Looper to draw a white pattern on the black lines. If you have a black-and-white screen, use the smallest eraser to draw loops on the black lines.

3. 

With the Rubber Stamp, apply an animal as your main symbol. You may see rabbits in the Ukrainian countryside. Paint the egg red. Use the Paint Can to color the ends and the middle of the egg red.

4.

Add some geometric designs with the Wacky Brush and Shapes and More Shapes.

5.

Flowers are often drawn on pysanky too. Draw flower patterns at both ends. Use the Paint Can to fill the flower petals with color.

Design Your Own Pysanky

You may want to design your own pysanky. Think of some symbols to represent long life, good health, and love. You can edit some Rubber Stamps to make those symbols or draw them with the Wacky Pencil. Select some Kid Pix Brush patterns and three or four colors to make the ribbon designs on your pysanky. You can print your drawing on paper and cut it out to give your pysanky to someone you love.

Dyeing Pysanky

You can make your own pysanky using eggs and dye. Ask an adult to do this activity with you.

Supplies

- uncooked chicken or duck eggs at room temperature
- old newspaper
- 1 sharp pin
- 1 bowl for egg white and yolk
- 4 bowls for dye
- egg carton
- yellow, blue, red, and black egg dye
- white wax crayon
- candle
- old, soft cloth

First, put newspaper on the table to catch spills. To empty each egg, slowly twirl the pin point in one end of the egg to make a hole about 1/8 inch wide. Turn the egg upside down over the bowl. Make a hole in the other end of the egg. Blow gently into one hole to force the egg white and yolk into the bowl. Rinse the empty egg in clear water. Set it in the egg carton to dry. Do the same for the rest of the eggs.

Prepare the dyes according to the instructions that come with the kit. Put one color in each small bowl. Let the dyes cool.

Firmly hold the hollow egg in the palm of one hand and "write" patterns on your egg with the white wax crayon. Press the crayon gently, but firmly, so you don't break the egg shell. Then dip the egg into the yellow dye. Remove it and let it dry in the egg carton.

Apply the second design and color. With the crayon "write" more of your design on the part of the egg shell that you want to remain yellow. Dip the egg into red dye. Yellow that is not covered with wax will turn orange with the red dye. Let the egg dry.

Repeat this process until you have used all four colors.

When the eggs are completely dry, remove the wax. Hold the egg next to the candle flame to soften the wax. Do not hold the egg above the flame, for it will turn the egg black from the smoke. Wipe the wax off with the old cloth. Now you will see your colorful designs!

GOOD-BYE CLOTH (Ghana)

Stamps made from squash? That's right! Fabric designers in Ghana carve stamp designs from calabash squashes. They dip the stamp in shiny black dye made from tree bark and press it on cloth strips.

Originally people wore clothes made of this fabric when they were attending the funeral of someone who had died or when they were leaving somebody's village. Ghanaians called the dye Adinkra which means good-bye. Named for the dye, people now call the stamped fabric Adinkra cloth, and they use white and colored material, not just black or brown that was used long ago. They hang Adinkra cloth on walls, use it as tablecloths, and sew it into clothing.

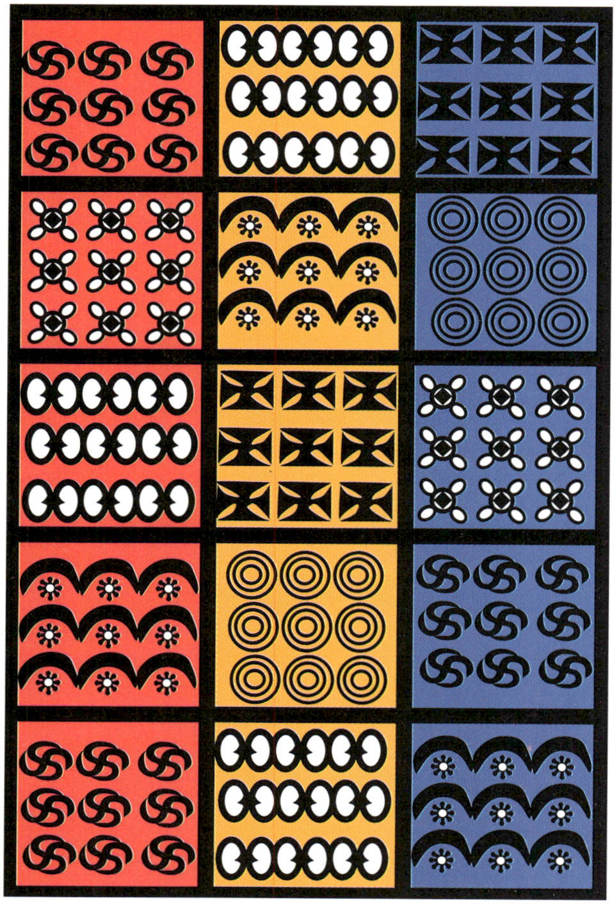

There are several steps to making Adinkra cloth. The artist carves pieces of calabash squash to make the stamp designs. He then paints squares on the cloth by dragging a comb dipped in dye across the material. Next he stamps several symbols in each square. After the cloth dries, the artist sews strips of the dyed fabric together with bright thread to make a larger piece. Because the symbols have traditional meanings and names, the finished Adinkra cloth gives a colorful message.

Create an Adinkra Cloth

Use Kid Pix to create some stamps and paint your own Adinkra cloth.

1. 

An important design is called Akoma, the symbol of patience. Create your own Akoma Rubber Stamp by modifying a Kid Pix stamp. Select the Rubber Stamp tool, then click on the heart stamp. Choose Edit Stamp from the Goodies menu. The Stamp Editor window will appear.

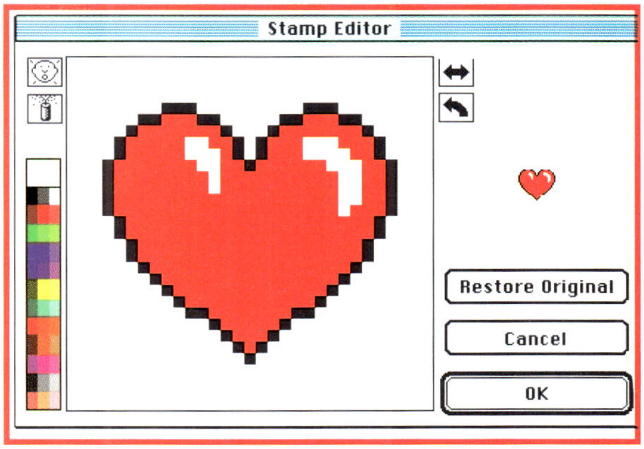

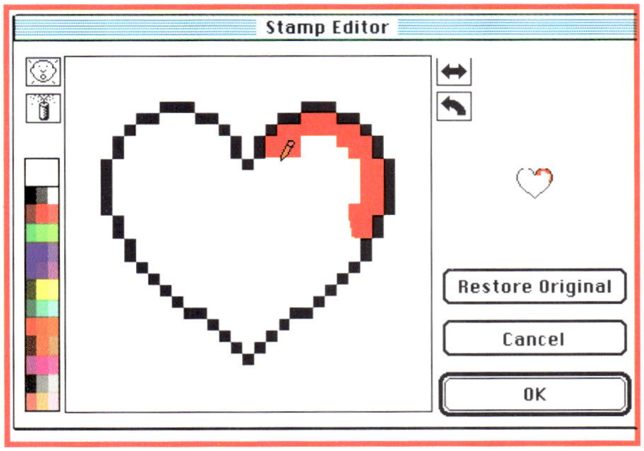

2.

With the little pencil in the Stamp Editor select white from the color palette. Click the pencil all over the red inside the heart to remove the color. If you make a mistake, click the Undo Guy in the Stamp Editor and try again.

3.

When you are satisfied with the stamp, click OK. Your new stamp will appear in the stamp palette.

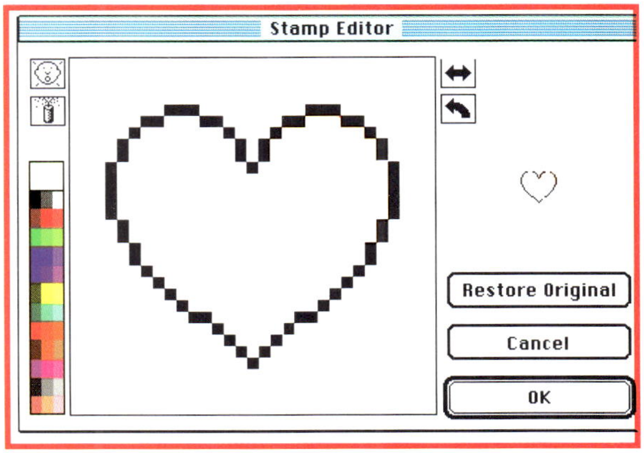

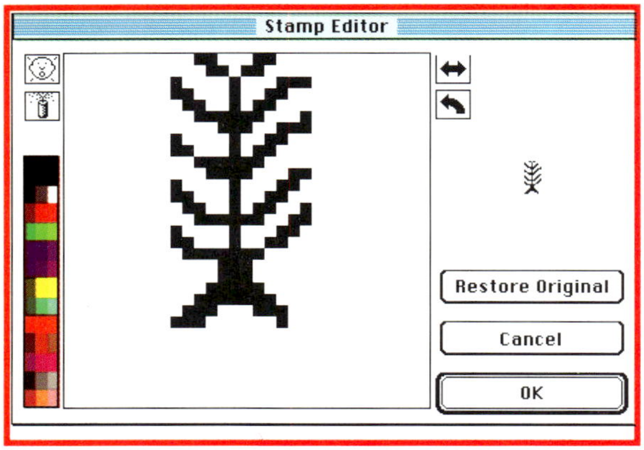

4. 

Now create a totally new Rubber Stamp. Choose another stamp and select Edit Stamp from the Goodies menu. This time, click on the firecracker in the upper left corner. The stamp will disappear. Use the Pencil and any color on the palette to draw another Adinkra stamp. Try making Aya, a fern that symbolizes defiance. If the stamp is not in the right position, click the arrows to move it. Click OK when you have finished drawing Aya.

5. 

Create some other Adinkra symbols with the Stamp Editor. Here are some examples:

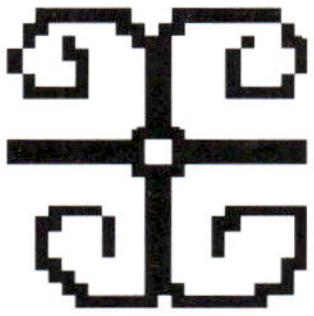

Dwanimen, ram's horns
Symbol of strength

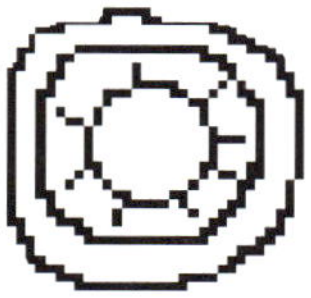

Adinkra 'hene
Symbol of royalty

Fihankra
Symbol of safety at home

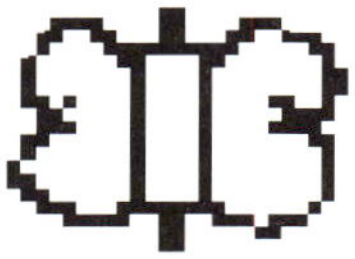

Hye wo nhye
Symbol of forgiveness

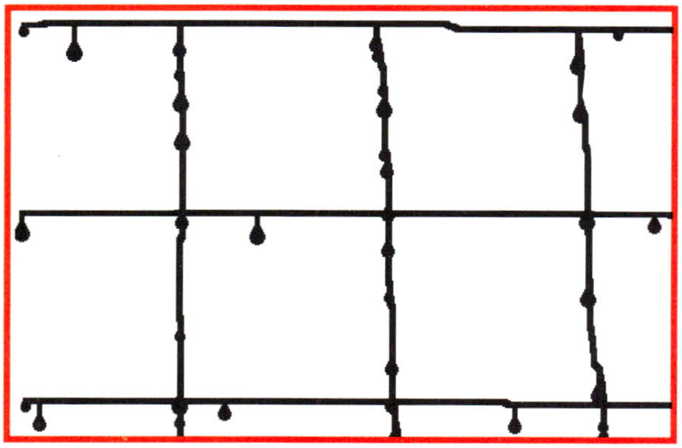

6. 

Design the cloth now. Instead of a comb, you can use the Kid Pix Wacky Brush and Drippy Paint to divide the fabric into squares. When you move the Wacky Brush quickly across the screen, there will be fewer drips. Try it. To make squares, draw three black drippy lines across your screen, and then draw three drippy lines down the screen.

7. 

The artist usually stamps a symbol several times in each square of Adinkra cloth. Decide what pattern you want, then stamp your symbols in each square to make traditional Adinkra cloth.

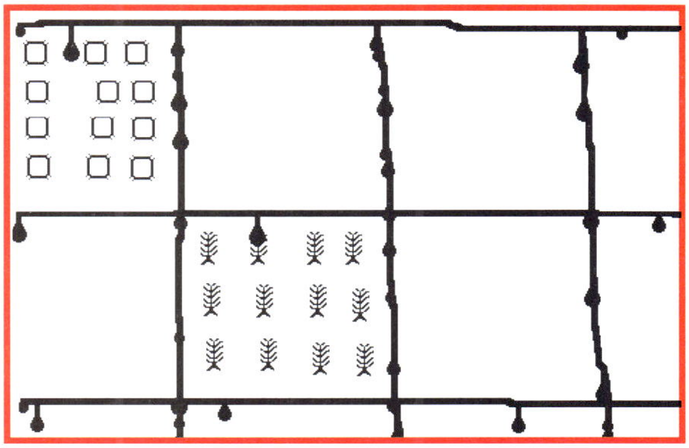

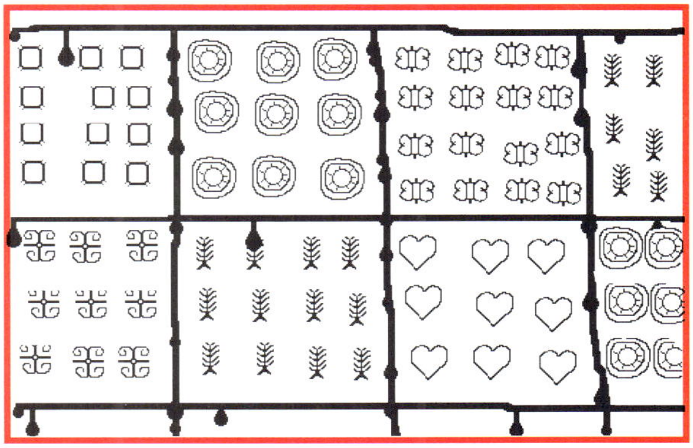

Design Your Own Adinkra Cloth

Make up your own symbols for different words or ideas. Use the Stamp Editor to create them. You can save your edited stamps in the Edit Stamp window by clicking on the OK button. If you're using a Macintosh, when you quit Kid Pix, a dialog box will appear asking if you want to save the stamp changes. If you want to keep your stamps, click on the Save button. If you're using a DOS or Windows version of Kid Pix, the program will automatically save your stamps. You can get the original Kid Pix stamps back whenever Kid Pix is running. Select the stamp that you changed, choose Edit Stamp, click on the Restore Original button, and then click on the OK button. The original Kid Pix stamp will appear in the stamp palette.

Now design your own version of Adinkra cloth. Print out your patterns and tape them together to make a wall hanging, wrapping paper, or book covers.

COOKIE STAMPS (Sweden)

Close your eyes and imagine the smell of cinnamon, cloves, and ginger. Picture yourself in a Swedish country kitchen, rolling spicy dough into thin sheets and cutting them into circles, diamonds, or squares to make scrumptious pepparkakor ginger snap cookies. Just before popping them into the oven to bake, you stamp designs on them with carved cookie stamps.

Men and boys in Sweden have enjoyed carving cookie stamps for more than three hundred years. Made of clay or wood, Swedish cookie stamps have animals, figures, hearts, flowers, or geometric patterns carved in them to make a design. Some designs are traditional for each province. They used to make the stamps during the long, cold winters when they had to stay indoors.

Young men carved stamps for their girl friends, who baked fiancé buns decorated with the stamps. Every family had a set of lovely stamps. They stamped beautiful designs on small holiday, wedding, and funeral cakes. When guests came to visit a Swedish home, they often left with cookies stamped with their host family's designs. Today many Swedish families use commercially made stamps. Some families still use and treasure stamps that were made by their ancestors long ago, and many kids in Sweden know the taste of pepparkakor.

Design a Swedish Cookie Stamp

With Kid Pix you can design a diamond-shaped cookie stamp.

1. 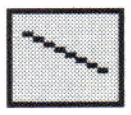

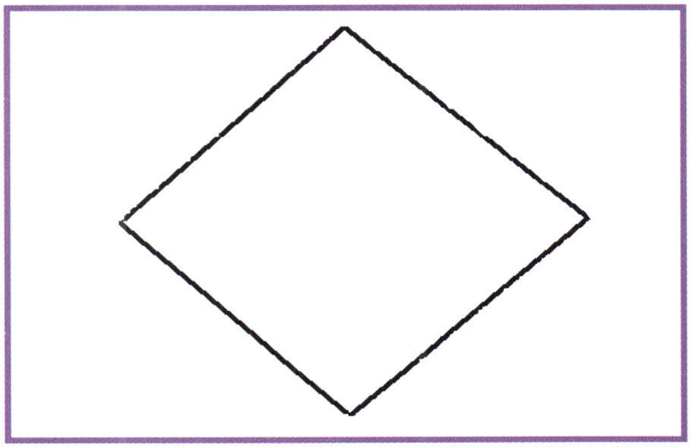

Use the Line to draw a large diamond shape. Click your mouse at the top center of the screen and drag the pointer to the middle right. Release your mouse. Click the mouse in the same spot and draw a line to the bottom center of the screen. Release your mouse. Click your mouse and draw a line from the bottom center to the middle left. Release your mouse, then draw a line from that point to the beginning of the first line.

2. 

Make a flower pattern inside the diamond. Use the Oval to draw a small circle in the center of the diamond. Hold down the Shift or Ctrl key as you drag the Oval. Next stamp a star in the center of the circle.

With the Wacky Pencil, draw eight petals of a flower around the circle.

3. 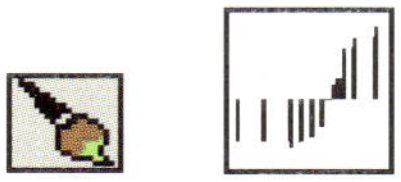

Swedish cookie stamps often had ridges carved into their flower petals. With Wacky Brush and Northern Lights, draw ridge patterns in each petal.

4. 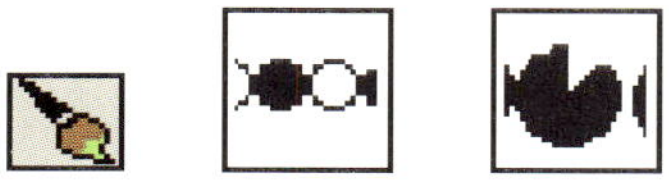

There often were patterns around the edges of the cookie stamps. Use Wacky Brush and Dots to make a nice edge trim.

Use Wacky Brush and Pie to finish off your design. Fill in the white spaces between the petals to complete your Swedish cookie stamp.

Create Your Own Cookie Stamp

Now that you know how to design a traditional cookie stamp, make up your own design. Decide what kind of pattern you want. You may want to use the same tools you used to create a traditional Swedish stamp to design a stamp of your own. Try using the Electric Mixer and Outliner to reverse your pattern.

Making Pepparkakor

When I was young, a Swedish student came to live with my family. She brought her mother's recipe for pepparkakor with her and told us that her family made these ginger snaps on St. Lucia's Day and on Christmas. On St. Lucia's Day, she came singing to each of us in our beds. Dressed in white and wearing a crown of candles on her head, she sang the song of St. Lucia. When we got out of bed, she treated us to pepparkakor she had made the night before. Here is her family recipe. Ask your parents or another adult to help you make these yummy ginger snaps.

Pepparkakor

Ingredients (This recipe makes about 250 small cookies)

2/3 cup dark corn syrup, slightly warm
1/2 cup soft butter or margarine
2/3 cup sour cream
1-1/2 cups sugar
1-1/2 teaspoons ground ginger
1 teaspoon ground cloves
2 teaspoons ground cinnamon
3 teaspoons baking soda dissolved in 2 tablespoons water
5 cups flour
margarine or oil

Mix all the ingredients except the flour in a large bowl. Gradually add 3-1/2 cups flour and mix thoroughly with a wooden spoon. Save the remaining 1-1/2 cups of flour for rolling out the dough. Cover the bowl and put it in the refrigerator overnight.

When you want to bake the cookies, preheat the oven to 400° F. Sprinkle flour on a pastry board to keep the dough from sticking. Roll out the dough with a rolling pin so it is about 1/4 inch thick. Cut out the cookies with cookie cutters or use a dull knife to cut square, round, or diamond shapes. Grease several cookie sheets with margarine or oil. Place the cookies on the sheets. If you have Swedish cookie stamps, stamp the designs on your cookies. Otherwise, press the back of a fork on each cookie to make a pattern. It will taste just as delicious!

Bake the cookies in the oven for 8 to 10 minutes. Let them cool on the cookie sheets before placing them on a cooling rack. Pop a pepparkakor in your mouth and savor the zingy, spicy flavor! M-m-m-m!

DREAMTIME (Australia)

Forty thousand years! That is how long Aborigines have been living in Australia. Before modern times they were nomads, traveling from place to place to hunt and gather food.

Like other native peoples, Aborigines record their history with pictures. They draw pictures of Dreamtime—a time when the world began and their Ancestral Beings gave them land and shaped the rocks, mountains, rivers, forests, deserts, plants, animals, and people and created the religious and social laws. Aboriginal paintings show animals and human beings and the places where they lived and traveled. Aborigines painted hunting and food gathering scenes, fights with other peoples, and religious ceremonies. Many paintings have circle, dot, and line patterns filling in the background, which may represent tracks of animals and humans traveling over land. Unlike dreams which are images that come to people in their sleep, Aborigines believe their Dreamtime was a real time in the history of their people.

The first drawings were made on rocks over thirty thousand years ago. As time passed, both men and women painted with different materials. They painted on eucalyptus tree bark with red and yellow ochre from the earth. Later, European settlers and missionaries gave the Aborigines paints and canvases. Today, some Aborigines use acrylic paints, wax resistant dyes, and even photography. Who knows, perhaps Aborigines will one day use Kid Pix to paint their Dreamtime.

Paint an Aboriginal Dreamtime

With Kid Pix tools you can paint a Dreamtime sea turtle.

1.  

Draw the turtle's head with the filled Oval. Use the Wacky Pencil to draw outlines of its shell and four flippers.

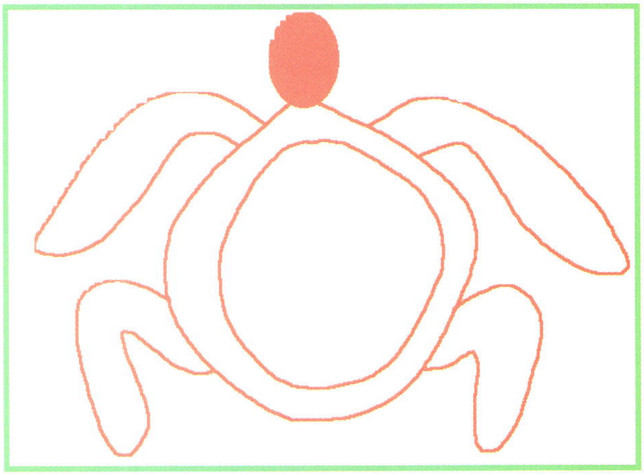

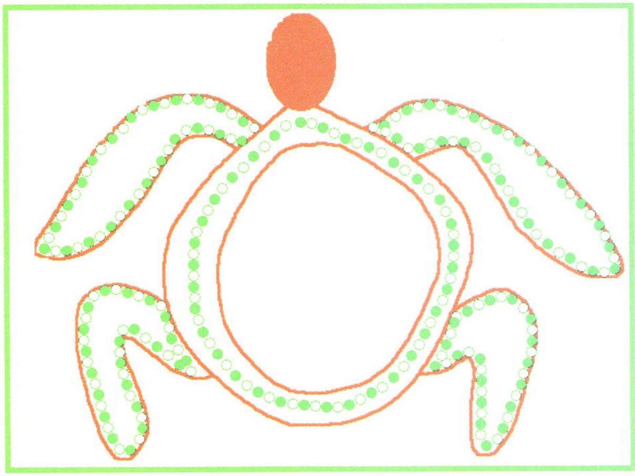

2.  

Aborigines often used dots to decorate animals. Use the Wacky Brush and Dots to decorate the turtle shell and flippers.

3.  

Dreamtime paintings are filled with patterns. Select the Paint Can and choose one of the fill patterns at the bottom of the screen. Pour patterns into the turtle flippers and shell. Oops! If your pattern spills all over the screen, quickly click the Undo Guy! There must be a leak somewhere. Find it and then use the Pencil to draw the lines together so there is no leak. Now pour with the Paint Can again to fill the turtle with the patterns.

4.  

Use the filled Oval to draw two eyes on the turtle head. Add some small white lines with the Wacky Pencil to make patterns.

5. 

Kid Pix has a great selection of patterns to fill the background of the Dreamtime painting. First use the Pencil to draw some lines from the turtle to the edge of the screen to divide the background into different parts. Be sure to connect the lines to the turtle outlines.

6.  

Now use the Paint Can and different patterns to complete the background of your Dreamtime painting. If the pattern spreads to places where you didn't want it to go, click the Undo Guy. Then use the Wacky Pencil to draw your background lines all the way from the edge of the turtle to the edge of the screen. Then there won't be a paint "leak." Fill the shapes with the Paint Can and patterns.

Paint Your Own Dreamtime Painting

Draw a Dreamtime painting with Kid Pix to record a time in your own history. Include animals and human beings. Fill in the background with different patterns. Try recording different events. Print it out and hang it on the wall.

EMBROIDERY (Greece)

Tulips, carnations, hyacinths, pomegranates, and artichokes—sounds like a flower, fruit, and vegetable stand! Guess again. Actually, these are common symbols in traditional Greek Island embroidery, a form of decorative stitching.

Young Greek girls living on islands in the Aegean Sea learned to use needle and silk thread to stitch patterns with names like Cretan feather, Romanian couching, satin, running, stem, cross, split, outline, flat, darning, chain, and fishbone. Women used dyes made from vegetables, herbs, and flowers to color the thread and washed it in sea water to keep the colors from running. They marked patterns of animals, plants, and people on pieces of paper and then carefully stitched the thread in designs on linen or cotton cloth.

Grandmothers and mothers taught the young girls how to embroider curtains, pillows, and sheets. Each girl also made and embroidered two dresses—one to wear at her own wedding and on festive occasions and the other to wear every day. Girls put these items in their dowry, the goods that a bride brought to her groom when they married.

Today some Greek Island girls use threads colored with commercial dyes to decorate their wedding dresses, but they still learn traditional embroidery from their mothers and grandmothers.

Practice Greek Embroidery Stitches

Kid Pix doesn't have needle and thread, but it does have some features that enable you to design your own embroidery patterns. First learn a few simple stitches.

1. 

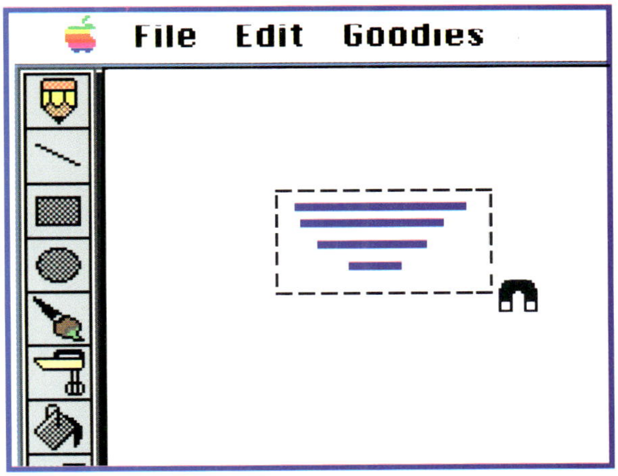

Practice the running stitch by making some triangle shapes for flowers. With a thin Line, draw four straight lines, one above the other. Each line is longer than the one before; this makes a triangle shape. Copy the design by selecting the Moving Van and Magnet. Drag the Magnet from a place to the left and above the pattern to a place to the right and below. Select Copy from the Edit menu. Then choose Paste from the Edit menu and click the mouse beside the first design.

2. 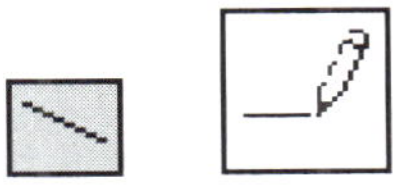

The satin stitch is very popular for flowers. Unlike the running stitch, satin stitches are sewn close together. Use the thin Line to make parallel stitches very close together in the shape of a tulip next to the first flowers.

3. 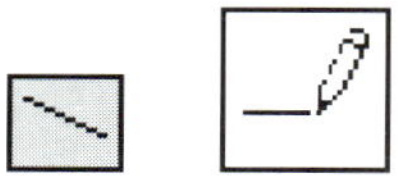

To make the stem stitch below the flowers, use the thin Line again to draw some very short straight lines one above the other. Try to make the lines the same length.

4. 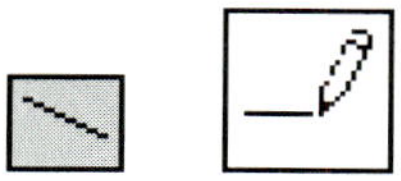

The split stitch makes a nice background pattern. In actual embroidery, the stitches enter and come out of the cloth in different places in each row. Use the thin Line and another color to make some grass with vertical lines of different lengths in a random pattern of long and short stitches.

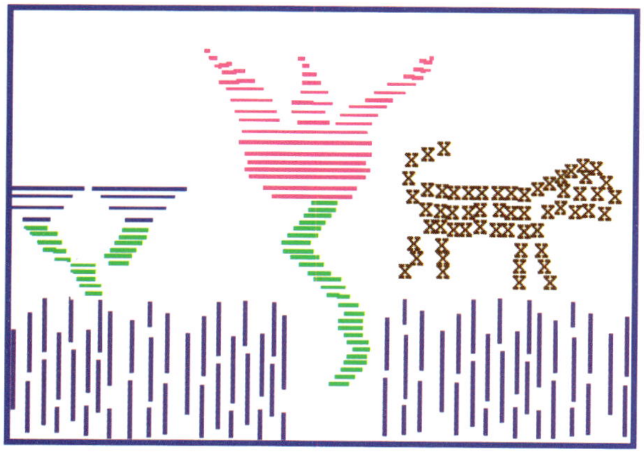

5. 

Alphabet Text can make a cross stitched figure or animal. Select Alphabet Text from the Goodies menu. When the dialog box appears, type a lot of x's in the Enter New Letters box. Click OK to close the box. Select Wacky Brush and Alphabet Line. Click the Alphabet x's on the screen to give your figure its shape. Don't worry if it isn't perfect. Greek Island girls had to practice a lot to master this skill.

6.  

Greek embroideries did not have too many empty spaces. Spaces between images were filled with background stitches, flowers, or small animals. Embroider some sky above the flowers and the cross stitched figure with the Wacky Brush and Looper to make a stitch that resembles the chain stitch. When you move the mouse slowly across the screen, the loops will be close together. When you move the mouse quickly, they will be further apart.

Make Your Own Embroidery Design

Draw a design for your own embroidery with Kid Pix and Wacky Pencil. Using Kid Pix tools and features you have learned in this and other activities, “stitch” your own Kid Pix embroidered picture. If you know how to embroider, you can print out your Kid Pix design and use it as a pattern to stitch it on cloth.

BEADWORK (United States)

Before European traders brought glass beads in the early 1800s, American Indian women used porcupine quills and other natural materials to decorate clothing and ornaments. Since that time Native Americans, as some American Indians prefer to be called, have decorated everything from clothes to cradles, utensils to bags, and horse saddles to war shields with glass beads.

Tribes in different regions developed distinctive beadwork styles. Woodland Indians of the Eastern United States, such as the Cree, beaded clothing with flower designs. The Crow often stitched triangles, rectangles, and diamonds with their beads. The Lakota made these patterns in light colored beads and added crosses and hourglass shapes. If you visit a Native American tribal ceremony today, you will see native people dressed in costumes decorated with beads.

In earlier times, women and girls sewed beads onto leather with sinew, a kind of "thread" made from animal tendons. Today, women, girls, men, and boys do traditional beadwork on clothing and other items using needle and thread. Men and boys decorate drums, ornaments, and instruments with beads, feathers, and bells. Some use a loom to weave beads into strips which they attach to clothes or make into necklaces and hair ornaments. Others stitch beads one by one to make designs for jewelry.

Design a Beaded Medallion

With Kid Pix tools, you can design your own Indian beaded medallion, which is a large medal or object shaped like a circle and worn as decoration.

1. 

Use the Rectangle filled with the color of leather to draw a thick stripe near the top of your screen. This will be the leather backing for your medallion.

2. 

Draw a circle filled with leather color in the center of the strip. Hold the Shift key down as you drag the Oval to make a perfect circle.

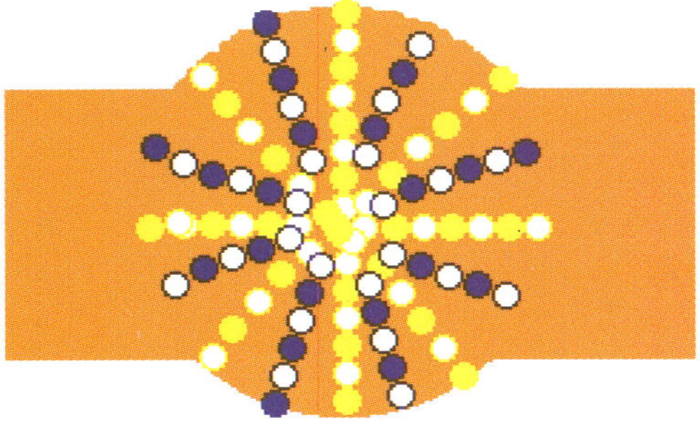

3.  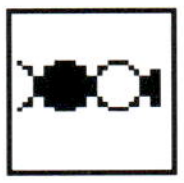

With Wacky Brush and Dots, bead the circle. Draw rays of colored beads from the center of the circle to the edges.

4. 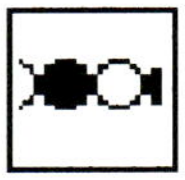

Fill in the spaces with another color of bead, using the Dots.

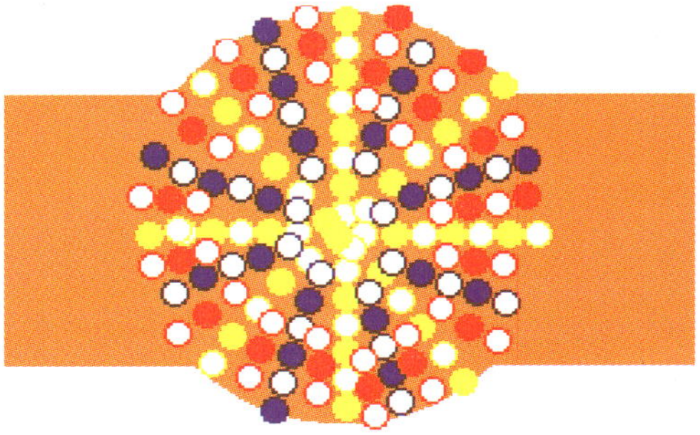

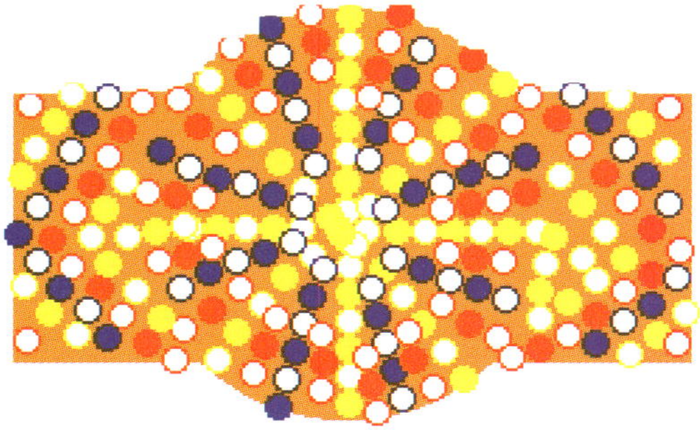

5. 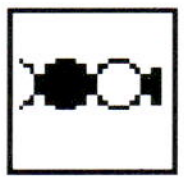

Now bead the sides of the medallion with rows of Dots.

6.  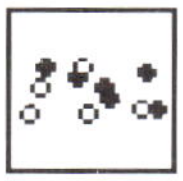

Use the Wacky Brush and Bubbly to finish off your medallion by drawing rows of tiny beads that dangle. The rows can be short or long and have different colored beads.

Wear a Beaded Medallion

To wear your medallion, save and print your drawing. Glue it to a piece of construction paper. Use scissors to carefully cut out the medallion. Glue a piece of colored ribbon on each end. Tie the ribbons around your neck and proudly show off your beaded design! When other kids ask you where you got your medallion, tell them you made it with Kid Pix!

MASKS (Around the World)

Have you ever wanted to look like something or somebody else? Wear a mask and maybe you can! Throughout history, people around the world have made and worn masks using different materials, including wood, paper, gourds, baskets, leather, cloth, and metal. They have decorated the masks with feathers, plants, animal horns, fur, beads, shells, and paint.

Masks have been worn for many different purposes and occasions. When buffalo roamed the American plains, Native Americans wore buffalo heads to disguise themselves when they hunted. Actors in Greece wore large masks so the audience could see them more easily. In Korea, actors still perform a mask dance drama with singing, dancing, and storytelling.

In many cultures, masks were made for spiritual purposes. People who wore them became the spirit or god displayed on the mask. Roman Catholic priests used to wear masks when they acted out religious stories. Inuit made animal spirit masks which they carried on sticks in front of them. Pacific Islanders wore masks to protect themselves from other spirits. Mexican Indians believe that wearing a mask enables them to be something other than an ordinary person. One of the most famous Mexican Indian masks is the Tigre, which means jaguar.

People also wear masks to teach traditions and to celebrate. In Zaire, boys are given masks when they are introduced to the ways of being men. Certain people in Mali wear the Chi Wara antelope mask in a ceremony performed when they plant seeds. Hopi Indians in North America make masks to honor the many friendly gods they call kachinas, for bringing corn and water to them. Children in the United States wear masks on Halloween when they visit neighbors and ask for treats.

Sometime in the 1400s, Italian actors created commedia dell'arte, which means comedy of art. They made up their dialogue as they performed the play. During these commedias, the actors wore dominos, which were half masks that cover only the eyes and forehead. Wouldn't it be fun to guess who was who by seeing only the person's nose, lips, and chin?

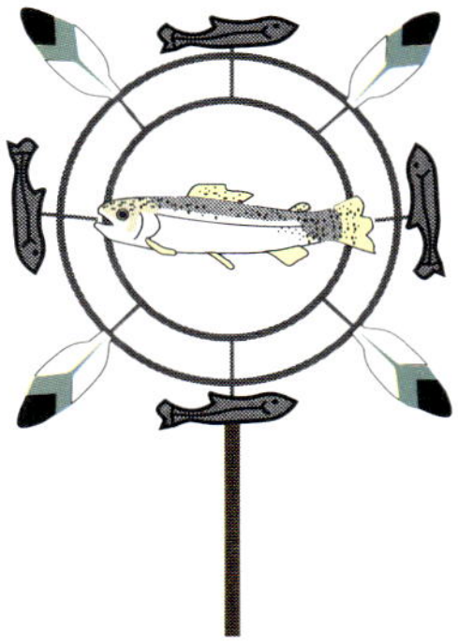

Draw a Mask

Kid Pix and the computer are great tools for creating dominos. A Kid Pix drawing is just about the right size for a half mask of a bird. This is a fantasy bird, so let your imagination soar.

1.

Draw the bird's beak in the center of the screen. Use Wacky Pencil to draw the outline. Use the Paint Can to fill it with color.

2.

Draw a circle for the center of its eyes. Hold down the Shift key and use the filled Oval to draw the first one. Use the Moving Van and Magnet to copy this circle and Paste it for the second eye.

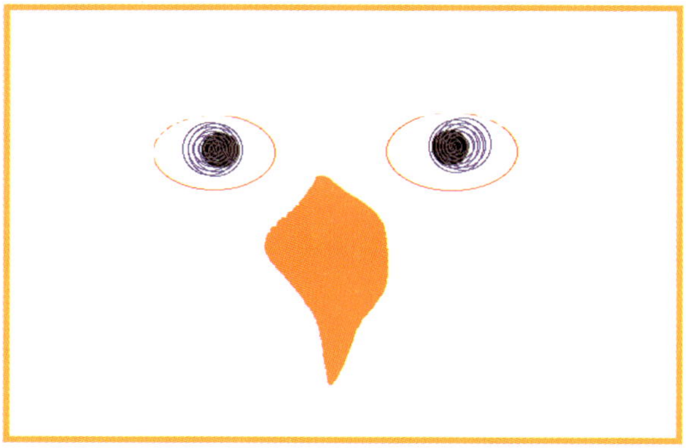

3. 

Add some circles within circles to the bird's eyes. Select Wacky Brush and Echoes. Click your mouse in the center of one eye and drag the mouse to one side until the circles go around the center of the eye. Select the Oval and another color and click on the first box on your left at the bottom of your screen. Draw an oval around each eye.

4. 

Now add some feathers to this bird's forehead. With the Wacky Pencil, draw a wide V shape from the top left edge down to the top of its beak and then up to the top right edge. Be sure the lines go all the way to the edge of the screen. Select the Paint Can. Select a feather fill pattern from the boxes at the bottom of your screen. Pour the feathers into the bird's forehead. Draw some feathers on its cheeks.

5. 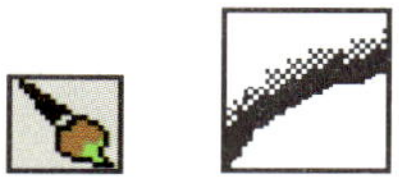

Add the small air holes above the beak. Use the Wacky Brush and 3D to make interesting shapes.

6. 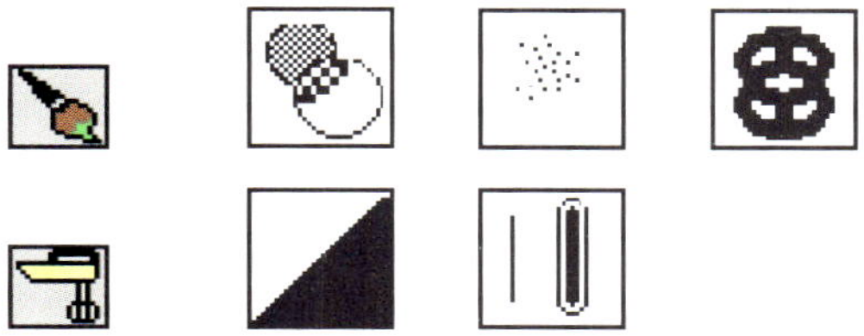

Decorate your bird mask using your favorite Kid Pix tools. The Wacky Brush and Magnifying Glass can make some of the feathers bigger. Spray Paint adds texture to the bird's face. Kaleidoscope can give your bird a colorful design. To change colors of your mask, see what happens when you use the Electric Mixer and Night and Day or Highlighter.

Wear a Domino

Save and print your bird drawing. Hold the drawing up to your face and ask someone to help you mark the position of your eyes with a crayon or marker. Move the mask away from your face and cut two holes with small scissors so that you can see through your mask. Trim the bottom edge of your mask with the scissors. Cut small holes near the top left and top right edges. Insert a piece of string in each hole and tie a simple knot. Use the strings to tie the mask around your head.

COLLAGE (Around the World)

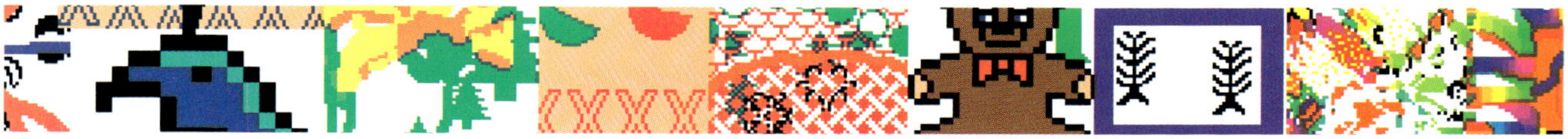

Mix and match. Snip, clip, and glue or paste. Putting bits of paper and other materials together and gluing them down is the art of collage. This word comes from the French word for glue, but Chinese people were making paper collage as early as 700 A.D. People from all over the world make different forms of collage. Masks made from bits of bone, beads, feathers, hair, teeth, and other objects attached to carved wood are a form of collage. Glued bits of stone, shells, or marble are another type of collage called mosaic.

The famous French artist, Picasso, made collage with paper, cloth, wood, metal, and sand. Other artists cut out photographs, bits of newspaper, small pieces of cloth, and colored tissue paper and glue them to large boards. School children make collages about their lives using baby photos, report cards, poems they have written, pictures they have drawn, and objects they have found.

A collage can be anything you like, as long as you have glue or paste!

Make a Kid Pix Collage

A lot of the fun in making a collage is collecting the materials to make it.

1.

Select New from the File menu to start a new drawing. A blank "page" will appear on your screen. Select Save from the File menu and type Collage in the name box. Click OK or Save. You will paste the pictures you collect into this file.

2. 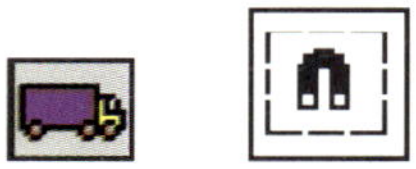

Now you can start collecting images from your Kid Pix drawings to put in your collage. Select Open from the File menu. Click on the name of the drawing you made in the Picture Story activity. Then click Open. Your drawing will appear on the screen.

Use the Moving Van and Magnet to select the rabbit in your drawing. Click the mouse and drag the cross from a spot to the upper left of the rabbits down and across the rabbits. Open the Edit menu and select Copy. Now select Close from the File menu. When the dialog box appears asking if you want to save changes to this drawing, click No.

3.

Kid Pix doesn't have glue, but it does have Paste! Here's how to use it. Open the Collage file you created in Step 1. Select Paste from the Edit menu. You can see the rabbits you copied. Your mouse cursor turns into a Paste jar. Place the Paste jar on the screen where you want your image to appear, then click your mouse. Choose Save from the File menu to save the additions to your drawing.

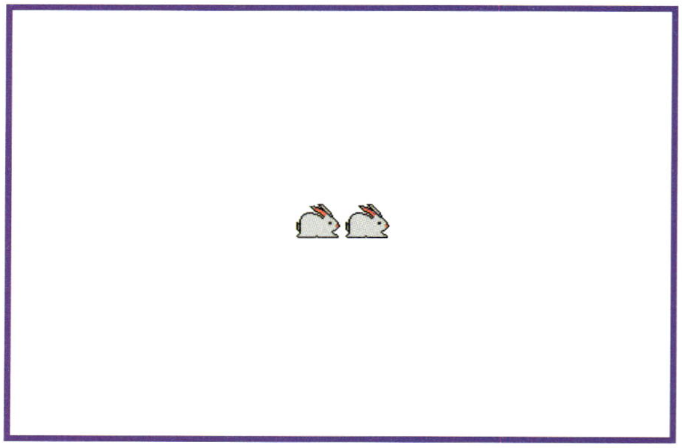

4.

Repeat steps 2 and 3 to copy parts of another drawing. You may want to copy some snowflakes from the Winter activity.

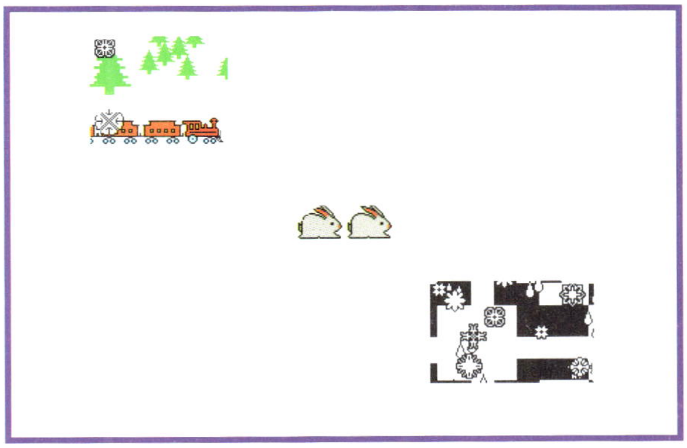

5.

Follow the same steps to include images from these activities: Kinglist Cloth, Good-Bye Cloth, Painted Walls, Cookie Stamps, Kamon, Patchwork Quilts, Masks, and Tiger Slippers.

Pieces of paper or other materials often overlap one another in a collage. You can paste parts of your drawings over parts of other drawings. For example, paste part of your Mask image over the Good-Bye image, or part of your Tiger Slipper over a corner of the Winter snowflakes. A collage is usually pretty full of images. If there are still large white spaces in yours, copy images from other drawings and paste them in.

Make a Paper Collage

If you haven't already done so, print out some of your Kid Pix drawings from other activities to use in making a paper collage. Use scissors to cut out parts of each drawing and set the cutout portions aside. After you have cut a good selection of images, bring out glue or paste and a large piece of construction paper. Think about how you want your paper collage to look. Experiment by laying the images out on the large paper without gluing them down. After you have decided where you want to place each image, paste them one by one onto the construction paper.

PEN PALS (Around the World)

Imagine that you really traveled around the world and made some new friends. Becoming pen pals is one of the best ways to keep in touch. Use Kid Pix to write a thank you note to an imaginary friend in Benin. Here's how.

1. 

Hold down the Option or Ctrl key and select the Text tool. Choose one of the eight fonts at the bottom of the screen by clicking on it. Now click the mouse on the screen where you want to begin typing.

If you don't know where all the letters are, look at the keyboard or ask an older person to help you. To type a capital letter, hold down the Shift key while you type the letter. When you finish typing a word near the right edge of the screen, press the Return key and continue typing.

2.

You might type a letter something like this to a friend in Benin:

Dear Pen Pal,

I had a very nice time visiting new people and places around the world.

Thank you for telling me about the old Fon kings and their giant umbrellas. They must have been very heavy!

Here is a drawing of my Kinglist cloth. I drew it with Kid Pix.

Come visit me soon!

Your friend,

Dear Pen Pal,

I had a very nice time visiting new people and places around the world.

Thank you for telling me about the old Fon kings and their giant umbrellas. They must have been very heavy!

Here is a drawing of my Kinglist cloth. I drew it with Kid Pix.

Come visit me soon!

Your friend,

Save your letter with the name Pal and then close it.

3.

Add some images from your Kinglist cloth drawing to the bottom of your letter. If you saved your drawing of the Kinglist cloth, open it now. Select the Moving Van and the Magnet and copy the ship from your drawing. Close the Kinglist cloth drawing without saving any changes.

Open the Pal letter. Select Paste from the Edit menu and Paste the ship at the bottom of your letter by clicking your mouse on the screen.

Dear Pen Pal,

I had a very nice time visiting new people and places around the world.

Thank you for telling me about the old Fon kings and their giant umbrellas. They must have been very heavy!

Here is a drawing of my Kinglist cloth. I drew it with Kid Pix.

Come visit me soon!

Your friend,

Dear Pen Pal,

I had a very nice time visiting new people and places around the world.

Thank you for telling me about the old Fon kings and their giant umbrellas. They must have been very heavy!

Here is a drawing of my Kinglist cloth. I drew it with Kid Pix.

Come visit me soon!

Your friend,

4. 

Do you remember which animal or plant you chose to represent you in your Kinglist cloth drawing? You can draw a small picture of it now at the bottom of your letter. You can use Wacky Pencil, Wacky Brush, or Rubber Stamps together or by themselves. For example, you can use the Pencil to add head plumes to the Rubber Stamp bird.

Save your letter and print it. If you don't remember how to print, or need help, read the section at the beginning of the book called "Around the World Toolkit."

Making Friends Around the World

People make friends around the world by exchanging letters and pictures. Here are some suggestions for finding a pen pal.

1. Write a letter to a relative who lives in another city or country.
2. Write to these organizations to find a pen pal:

   World Pen Pals, 1694 Como Avenue, St. Paul, MN, USA 55104

   International Friendship League, 55 Mount Vernon Street, Boston, MA, USA 02108

   U.S. Postal Service Olympic Pen Pal Club, P.O. Box 9419, Gaithersburg, MD USA 20898-9419
3. Ask your teacher to find a school in another city or country with children who would like to be pen pals with the kids in your class.

4. If you belong to a service or religious group, ask the elders to help you organize a pen pal project with children of the same organization in another town or country.

5. Almost every country has an office, called an embassy, in the United States. If you would like to exchange letters with children in a particular country, write a letter to the embassy of that country asking them for help in setting up a pen pal exchange. Your local librarian can help you find the address of the embassy.

6. Look in the local phone book under Fraternal Organizations and get the names and phone numbers of groups in your area. The Rotary Club has an international branch that sponsors student exchange programs. Other clubs also support international programs. Call them and ask if they can put you in touch with young people who would like a pen pal.

Half the fun of traveling around the world is keeping friends throughout your life!

GLOSSARY

Aborigine (ah-bo-RI-jean-ee) When capitalized, the name given to native peoples living in Australia. When not capitalized, means native peoples living in any part of the world.

Adinkra (ah-DIN-kra) Ghanaian word for good-bye.

Agonglo (Ah-GON-glo) A Fon king whose name means "pineapple impossible" because he saved himself by holding onto a pineapple when he was attacked by his enemies.

Akoma (AH-ko-ma) Ghanaian word for heart and symbol for patience.

Alps A range of high mountains stretching across Switzerland, with many peaks more than 10,000 feet high. From the Latin word "alb," which means white.

American Indians Indigenous people of North America. Also known as Native Americans.

appliqué (AP-pli-kay) A method of stitching pieces of fabric onto larger pieces of cloth. The edges of the small pieces are turned under and sewn on with tiny stitches.

Aya (I-ya) Ghanaian word for fern, symbol of defiance.

canción (kahn-see-ON) Spanish word for song. Plural is canciones.

Chi Wara (chee WAH-ra) A magical being of the Bambara people in Mali, West Africa, who came to earth as an antelope to teach the Bambara agriculture. Honored in carved wooden headdresses and dance to bring bountiful harvest.

collage (ko-LAJZ) French word describing a composition made of different materials, including paper and found objects which are glued onto another material.

Commedia dell 'arte (ko-MAID-dee-ya dell-ART-ay) Italian for "comedy of art," a form of theater which involves spontaneous dialogue. Actors often wear half masks called dominos during the performance.

domino (DAH-mee-no) Italian word for the half mask worn by performers during a commedia dell 'arte. The domino covers the upper half of the face, leaving the nose, mouth, and chin exposed.

Dwanimen (DWAHN-ee-mun) Ghanaian word for ram's horns, symbol of strength.

elefante (el-ay-FAHN-te) Spanish word for elephant.

Eskimo (ES-kee-mo) The name that American and Canadian Indians called the people living in the far northern part of the Arctic. This name was commonly used by Europeans who visited or settled in the Arctic. Some Arctic people prefer to be called Inuit.

Fon (FAHN) The royal court in Benin during the time before Benin was colonized.

fukusa (foo-koo-sah) A small, decorated silk scarf which Japanese people use to wrap a gift for a special occasion, such as a wedding. Sometimes has kamon printed on it. (Japanese words do not have accented syllables.)

Gangnihessou	(Gahn-nee-HES-oo) The first Benin Fon king, whose name means "chief is male bird" in their language.
Haida	(HI-dah) Name of a Pacific Northwest Coast tribe.
Inuit	(IN-oo-it) The name Eskimos call themselves. It means "the people" in their language.
kachinas	(ka-CHEE-nahs) Friendly gods honored by Hopi Indians in the United States for bringing them corn and rain. Hopi parents make kachina dolls to teach their children about their cultural customs and traditions.
kamon	(kah-mon) Japanese family crest.
kimono	(kee-mo-no) Japanese loose, wide-sleeved robe, worn with a broad sash.
kinglist cloth	(king-list) Colorful, appliqued cloths originally made by tailors for the Fon kings in Benin.
kistka	(KISST-kah) A tiny funnel with a handle used by Ukrainians to decorate psyanky.
krashanky	(krah-SHAHN-kee) Dyed hardboiled eggs which are eaten at Easter by people in Ukraine.
Kwakiutl	(Kwah-key-OO-til) Name of a Pacific Northwest Coast tribe. Famous for the Thunderbird's performance in the Kwakiutl Winter Ceremonial.
Lixia	(lee-shee-AH) Chinese holiday celebrated on the fifth day of the fifth month.
Ming dynasty	Periods in Chinese history were characterized by their rulers' families. The Ming dynasty lasted 276 years from 1368 through 1644.
Native Americans	Indigenous people of North America who belong to different tribes, including Shoshone, Crow, Hopi, Zuni, and Lakota. Also known as American Indians.
Nyame Biribi wo soro	(Nee-O-may bee-ree-bee wo so-ro) Ghanaian word for hope.
origami	(o-ree-gah-mee) Japanese paper-folding craft.
pájaro	(PA-ha-ro) Spanish word for bird.
pepparkakor	(pep-per-KAH-kor) Swedish spice cookie with ginger flavor.
Persians	(PER-see-ahns) People of ancient Persia are called Persians. This country is now called Iran, and its citizens Iranians.
pysanky	(pih-SAHN-kee) Brightly colored eggs that are decorated with melted beeswax and dye and exchanged by the people of Ukraine at Easter time. From the verb, pysaty.
pysaty	(pih-SAH-tee) Ukrainian for the verb "to write."
samurai	(sa-moo-rah-ee) In ancient Japan there was a class of people called samurai. They were the warriors who fought on behalf of the Japanese warlords.
Tlingit	(TLING-git) Name of a Pacific Northwest Coast tribe. Well-known for their Frog crest.
totem	(TO-tem) An animal, plant, or other natural object that serves as an emblem of a family or clan because of a special ancestral relationship.
Tsimshian	(SIM-shahn) Name of a Pacific Northwest Coast tribe.
umiak	(OO-mee-ahk) Large boat about eight feet wide and thirty feet long, made from tree saplings and walrus skins, used by Inuit for hunting and fishing.

FURTHER READINGS

Check your local bookstore or library for these and other books and magazines about peoples around the world.

Books

Children's Atlas of Native Americans. Chicago: Rand McNally, 1992.

Children's Atlas of the World. Chicago: Rand McNally, 1991.

Portraits of the Nations Series: The Land and People of (Country, etc.). New York: HarperCollins, 1991.

The World and Its Peoples. New York: Greystone Press, 1964.

Totem Poles to Cut Out and Put Together. Santa Barbara: Bellerophon Books, 1988.

Visual Geography Series, (Country) in Pictures. Minneapolis, Lerner Publications, 1989.

Adams, Monni, "Fon Appliqued Cloths," *African Arts* magazine, Feb. 1980.

Birket-Smith, Kaj. *Eskimos.* New York: Crown Publishers, 1971.

Bradshaw, Angela. *World Costumes.* London: Adam and Charles Black, 1952.

Brown, Fern G. *Valentine's Day.* New York: Franklin Watts, 1983.

Cohen, Hennig and T. P. Coffin. *The Folklore of American Holidays.* Detroit: Gale Research, 1987.

Cole, Ann, and C. Haas, E. Heller, and B. Weinberg. *Children Are Children Are Children.* New York: Little Brown, 1978.

Comins, Jeremy. *Latin American Crafts and Their Cultural Backgrounds.* New York: Lothrop, Lee and Shepard, 1974.

Comins, Jeremy. *Totems, Decoys and Covered Wagons—Cardboard Constructions from Early American Life.* New York: Lothrop, Lee and Shepard, 1976.

Corwin, Judith Hoffman. *African Crafts.* New York: Franklin Watts, 1990.

Courtney-Clarke, Margaret. *African Canvas, the Art of West African Women.* New York: Rizzoli, 1990.

D'Amato, Janet and Alex. *African Crafts for You to Make.* New York: Julian Messner, 1969.

Feelings, Tom. *Moja Means One.* New York: Dial, 1971.

Green, Paul and A. Abbott. *I am Eskimo, Aknik My Name.* Juneau: Alaska-Northwest Publishing, 1959.

Halliburton, Richard. *Complete Book of Marvels.* Indianapolis: Bobbs-Merrill, 1960.

Johnson, Lois S. *Happy New Year Round the World.* Chicago: Rand McNally, 1966.

Joseph, Joan. *Folk Toys Around the World.* New York: Parents' Magazine Press with U.S. Committee for UNICEF, 1972.

Kalman, Bobbie. *Japan the Culture.* New York: Crabtree Publishing,1989.

Kerina, Jane. *African Crafts.* New York: Lion, 1970.

Lester, Julius. *Black Folktales.* New York: Grove Press, 1969.

Mann, Shiah. *Chinese New Year.* New York: A.R.T.S., 1976.

Morris, Neil. *The Children's Illustrated Activity Atlas.* Milwaukee: Gareth Stevens Children's Books, 1989.

Ortiz, Simon. *The People Shall Continue.* Emeryville: Children's Book Press, 1977.

Perl, Lila. *Ghana and Ivory Coast, Spotlight on West Africa.* New York: William Morrow, 1975.

Purdy, Susan and C. R. Sandak. *A Civilization Project Book: Eskimos.* New York: Franklin Watts, 1982.

Schuman, Jo Miles. *Art From Many Hands, Multicultural Art Projects For Home and School.* Englewood Cliffs: Prentice Hall, 1981.

Stepanchuk, Carol and C. Wong. *Mooncakes and Hungry Ghosts, Festivals of China.* San Francisco: China Books and Periodicals, 1991.

Steptoe, John. *Mufaro's Beautiful Daughters.* New York: Lothrop, Lee and Shepard Books, 1987.

Viola, Herman J. *After Columbus, The Smithsonian Chronicle of the North American Indians.* Washington, D.C.: Smithsonian Institute, 1990.

Warren, Jean and E. McKinnon. *Totline Small World Celebrations.* Everett: Warren Publishing House, 1988.

Yee, Paul. *Tales from Gold Mountain, Stories of the Chinese in the New World.* New York: MacMillan,1989.

Periodicals

Cobblestone

Cricket Magazine

Daybreak Star Reader

Faces

Spark!

EVERY KID PIX NEEDS A COMPANION!

Order Kid Pix Companion now and save 25%. With Kid Pix Companion™, you'll add these exciting new features to Kid Pix™: Slide Show™, DrawMes™ and ColorMes™, plus 112 great new Rubber Stamps and 19 new Hidden Pictures.

What's more, many of the Rubber Stamps are multicultural! So you can have even more fun with ***Kid Pix Around the World!***

Visit your favorite software dealer. Or save 25% by using the order form below or by calling 1-800-521-6263. Mention special offer #233.

Save 25% by using this order form, or by calling Brøderbund Software-Direct at 1-800-521-6263.

Item No.	Description	Qty.	Regular Price	Special Price	Total
28055	Kid Pix - Mac		$59.95	$44.95	
27412	Kid Pix - DOS		$59.95	$44.95	
27402	Kid Pix - Windows		$59.95	$44.95	
28302	Kid Pix Companion - Mac*		$39.95	$29.95	
28301	Kid Pix Companion - DOS*		$39.95	$29.95	
				Sub Total	
				Shipping & Handling	$4.00
				Sales Tax*	
				Grand Total	

*Requires Kid Pix

To order send this order form with payment to:
Brøderbund Software-Direct Special Offer #233
P. O. Box 6125
Novato, CA
94948-6125

Brøderbund

*Local sales tax must be added in the following states: AZ, CA, GA, IL, MA, MN, PA, TX. Please include the appropriate sales tax for your state. Allow 4 weeks for delivery.

No-Risk Money-Back Guarantee!
If you are not completely satisfied, return the package and contents within 60 days along with a copy of your invoice or packing slip. We'll promptly refund your money.

Name ____________________ Address ____________________

City ____________ State ______ Zip ______ Daytime Phone ____________

Type of Payment ____________ Exp. Date ____________ Signature ____________

We accept American Express, Visa, Master Card, Checks and Money Orders